"Michael Prosserman has written in his authentic voice, a timely book about the importance of determination, creativity, and vulnerability in leadership . . . and in life. A grassroots triumph!" — SHARON AVERY, President & CEO of Toronto Foundation

"He endures high levels of anxiety around every corner, the son of a schizophrenic mother and a father suffering from Parkinsons. To describe him as an average student would be charitable and with three fused vertebrae in his neck, the notion of an athletic career should have been a non-starter. 'Piecez' defied the odds and became world renowned in the breakin' world (break dancing for the rest of us). Perhaps a hero to some. That is not what defines his alter ego Michael Prosserman, who has stepped up and built Unity, a non-profit that uses breakin' to reach teens in underserved communities, building values, self-esteem, and leadership. His philosophy, embodied in his new marvellous book, can be summarized in one line: "our work was about contribution not attribution." His humility and honesty make *Building Unity* a worthy read. A great reminder for all of us." — NORMAN BACAL, best-selling author of *Odell's Fall* and *Breakdown*

"The world we live in is transforming before our eyes in extraordinary ways. To help our divided communities begin to heal, we need people like Mike Prosserman. Mike's vulnerability and passion for his work comes through in every word. As you read his unique story, you'll witness the kind of perseverance we all wish for when tackling our own challenges — and you'll be surprised at how much you learn about hip hop culture along the way. Read this book and get inspired to make a difference in *your* world." — KEN BLANCHARD, coauthor of *The New One Minute Manager*® and *Servant Leadership in Action*

"A powerful and personal biography, with a lesson for all of us on each page. Brave, poignant, and practical, an inspiring road map for a new generation of leaders." — SETH GODIN, author of *This is Marketing*

"Mike Prosserman lived by the motto: *Think Big, Start Small, and Scale Up* to establish Unity Charity. It is extraordinary that he began this life trajectory at fifteen. I'm sending you a Unity hug. Remember I was the Grandma." — SHARON JOHNSTON, wife of former Governor General David Johnston AKA Unity Grandma

"An inspiring testimony from a super kind and generous leader — who knew what he wanted from the ripe young age of 15 — as he smiles through the tears of Building Unity. He hasn't changed one bit while always looking forward!! My heart and eyes smiled and danced while reading, thanks Mike!" — MICHIE MEE, award-winning Canadian Hip Hop icon and actor

"I don't know Mike P. I don't know Unity. But when I started reading this book I couldn't stop. Ready to make your dent in the world but don't know where to start? Right here. This book. I think it will leave you chomping at the bit to get going like it did for me." — NEIL PASRICHA, author of *The Book of Awesome* and host of *3 Books* podcast

"Mikey 'Piecez' Prosserman's journey and dedication to making this world a better place through Hip Hop is truly inspiring. And if there is anything I took personally from reading *Building Unity*, it's that applying the b-boy mentality to life can help your career from being an innovator, creating something from nothing, and constantly evolving. A true testimony that hard work never goes unnoticed." — B-BOY RONNIE, Red Bull Dancer, Super Cr3w

"Unity shows the deepest forms of community strength and the hardships of what a child of culture can be capable of due the exact facts of growing up in a street/urban culture. A must read and a story to be motivated from." — B-BOY THESIS, Knuckleheads Cali, Massive Monkees

"As a 41-year-old b-boy, I never liked to read until I got into *Building Unity*. The lessons that B-boy Piecez explains are so on point, I wanted to call him after every chapter I read to pick his brain even more. I am truly inspired by his stories about his family, how he got his name, and his non-profit, and every time I think about *Building Unity* it reminds me of an owner's manual. *Building Unity* is an educational tool for the breaking scene." — B-BOY WICKET

"This is a handbook to spark the critical thought process of how one can be of service to their community. Through a step-by-step process and shared narrative, the reader can learn how to turn their thoughts into actions! Great work!" — YNOT, Rock Steady Crew

"'Piecez' pieces poetry and practical and people perfectly. Turns tragedy into tales and tales into tell-all tips of Building Unity — the charity and the movement. This is an on-its-head 'how to' with enough tools and tricks for anyone wanting to spark and build and grow a non-profit from idea to go. And enough rhythm, room, and groove for *you* to lead as only *you* can. Authentic, vulnerable, uplifting, spinning, effortless, epic. Just like Prosserman — one of the hardest working servant leaders I know." — DANIELE ZANOTTI, President & CEO of United Way Greater Toronto

BUILDING UNITY

BUILDING UNITY

Leading a Non-Profit from
Spark to Succession

MICHAEL "PIECEZ" PROSSERMAN

Published by ECW Press
665 Gerrard Street East
Toronto, Ontario, Canada M4M 1Y2
416-694-3348 / info@ecwpress.com

"On Children" by Khalil Gibran, quoted on page 205 from *The Prophet* (Knopf, 1923). This poem is in the public domain.

Cover design: David Drummond
Illustrations: © Caerina Abrenica
Original diagram on page 106 by Roman Lifshitz

LIBRARY AND ARCHIVES CANADA CATALOGUING IN PUBLICATION

Title: Building unity : leading a non-profit from spark to succession / Michael "Piecez" Prosserman.

Names: Prosserman, Michael, author.

Identifiers: Canadiana (print) 20200233858
Canadiana (ebook) 20200234005

ISBN 978-177041-563-8 (softcover)
ISBN 978-1-77305-607-4 (PDF)
ISBN 978-1-77305-606-7 (EPUB)

Subjects: LCSH: Nonprofit organizations—Management. LCSH: Organizational effectiveness. | LCSH: Leadership.

Classification: LCC HD62.6 .P76 2020
DDC 658.4/092—dc23

The publication of *Building Unity* has been funded in part by the Government of Canada. *Ce livre est financé en partie par le gouvernement du Canada.* We also acknowledge the contribution of the Government of Ontario through Ontario Creates for the marketing of this book.

ONTARIO CREATES   Canada

PRINTED AND BOUND IN CANADA   PRINTING: FRIESENS   5 4 3 2 1

MIX
Paper from
responsible sources
FSC
www.fsc.org   FSC® C016245

To my mom, Michelle; my dad, Ron; my wife, Melissa; and my dog, Olive
— the pillars of my life and the foundation of my resilience.

In memory of my late therapist, Dr. Joseph Regan, who saved my life.
You will be remembered forever.

CONTENTS

INTRODUCTION

This book is about building something that didn't exist, something that would bring about new forms of justice, something I doubted I could really build until I began to see it coming together in front of my eyes, one small piece at a time. This is not a book about failing fast or testing things quickly and moving on if they don't work. In fact, it's the opposite; it's about slow, heart-wrenching, long-term growth through dedicated work and believing in something at its very core. It's about loyalty. It's about sticking around for something you believe in so deeply that you don't just give up on it when it doesn't work out the first time or even the second time. It is not about hacks or shortcuts. It is about perseverance and always learning.

The idea of making the world a better place can be problematic. Sometimes our good intentions can lead to unintended damaging results. But I believe the work we do, our words, and actions can be transformative. The journey of learning is constant with the communities we aim to serve.

For me, the process of discovery and reflection was constant. The intersection of identity, strength, and skill was the spark that turned an idea into reality. Our team at Unity "flipped" impact: learning the foundation of how to do something and then making it our own by adding our style to it. We need innovative ideas to address the world's most pressing problems — flipping impact to match the need of the communities we serve while challenging the status quo.

This book includes flexible frameworks and stories of how we created the most responsible impact we could as a team of community-minded hip-hop artists. It acts as a window into my learning journey as a b-boy and an entrepreneur, a view to how creativity on the dance floor paralleled my progress building an organization with social purpose.

I try to use plain language and avoid buzzwords. This is not about complex theories. It's about practice and self-reflection. Throughout my storytelling, I've compiled learnings, practical tools, and reflection questions to support you on your journey. Our team created something out of nothing, just as we do in hip hop. We led with our hearts and learned the hard way.

I invite you to take any of these ideas and lessons and remix them to make them yours. Flip them. To me that's the common thread between breakin' and entrepreneurship. Take a pre-existing idea and flip it into something new, something relevant to your story, your experience, your context.

In breakin' there is a foundational move called the *Six Step*. By no coincidence, this book's structural framework comprises the six steps we took in growing Unity, the six pillars that have been my foundation for turning ideas into community-driven impact:

1. Spark: hip hop + mental health
2. Build: building the plane while flying it
3. Trust: crews and cyphers

4. Grow: planting seeds for the future
5. Evolve: steps to succession
6. Re-Ignite: launching EPIC

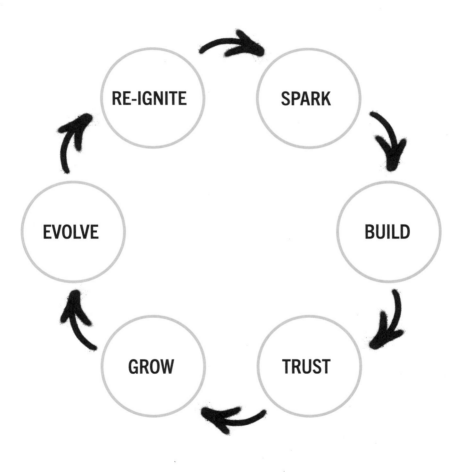

This image captures my journey of building Unity from the ground up. It mirrors elements of my creative process on the dance floor. It is a process of discovery. After working with a wide variety of clients, I began to realize there are common threads in the journey of discovering impact. The process of building Unity was highly contextual and nuanced. The environment in which we worked was constantly changing and we needed to be responsive, so our approach could never be linear or follow a one-size-fits-all model; it was always evolving. I began to realize it was a process of discovery, reflection, and constant learning. Always challenging ourselves to do better. Ultimately, it was something we needed to do to understand. Experience was our teacher.

I'm sharing this framework not as a linear solution, but as a flexible lens through which to discover impact. There are reflection questions at the end of each chapter to give you the opportunity to reflect on your impact. Challenge yourself, push your limits, move the dial. Every action matters and there is no action too small.

While we built Unity, we were constantly discovering the way forward based on the strengths of our team, while taking the time to reflect on the impact we were having and how we could do better. This helped us discover and fill gaps, and we did our best to apply learning in real time. Reflection helped uncover barriers, challenge assumptions, and create space to address issues. Reflecting on our impact every step of the way helped us understand how we could be responsive and better serve our communities. We built the plane while flying it.

FLIPPING IMPACT

Hip hop culture is a metaphor for life, leadership, and innovation. It has some powerful and universal philosophies and lessons to pull from. I applied the values I took from hip hop to my process in building Unity from the ground up.

In hip hop, when someone does a move that inspires me, I "flip it." To *flip* something is to build on someone else's idea or innovate a common concept that has been done before. I take inspiration from what I see on the dance floor or learn from my peers and add to it from my own experiences and strengths: I flip it. Instead of starting from scratch, to flip something you first seek knowledge and then add new ideas based on your own story, creativity, personality, and context. Understanding the basics enables you to build from strengths while identifying weaknesses and filling gaps. It is a constant process of discovery through doing paired with critical reflection on how to always do better.

It's not copying others' ideas or recreating something that already exists in the world. It's about innovating from the foundation of a concept rather than trying to reinvent the wheel. I acknowledge history and ideas that came before me while adding my own unique flavour and style. I work to understand the ecosystem in order to figure out where new ideas might be needed, to identify the existing ways of doing things that are no longer relevant, and then I add something new. Flipping an idea creates space to innovate.

Breakin' is a culture that respects learning, the idea of always being a student and seeking knowledge from other members of the community. It is incredibly adaptive and nimble. Unlike in traditional education, there is no formal system to teach the foundation. Knowledge is passed down from mentors, crews, peer exchanges at practice sessions, and from elders. In breakin', this is often referred to as "each one teach one": dancers take what they learn and add their own unique style, flipping ideas to make them relevant to their personality and way of telling their stories — how they express themselves and speak their truth. This is in direct contrast to *biting*, which is highly frowned upon in breakin'. Biting is copying someone else's unique moves exactly, and it is completely disrespectful to the originators of those moves.

Flipping is also an opportunity to transform a negative into a positive. This is done in hip hop culture, because people often find themselves in situations where they must build something out of nothing. It is about transforming or flipping these situations with a strong will and hard work and by denying the path that others set for you. It is even used in slang in hip hop. We often say words like "bad," "ill," "sick," and "dope" to describe something good. We flip negative words to describe something positive.

Flipping ideas directly parallels my creation process at Unity. I learned everything I could about how to start a non-profit and then built Unity with our team, drawing on all our strengths to do so. We filled gaps constantly as we identified areas in which we needed to learn more. When we felt the pressure to grow without the right knowledge, we gathered information in any way we could. Instead of starting from scratch, we tried to learn from what was out there, flip it, and make it our own. It was a constant process of discovery and reflection, flipping what we learned into new ways of doing things, building from a foundation of non-profit sector knowledge. We flipped boards of directors, flipped fundraising, flipped leadership. The cycle continued. We learned, we flipped, we grew.

Throughout the book I will reference how we "flipped" impact, leadership, operations, and all functional areas of running an organization. How we took inspiration from mentors in areas like finance, fundraising, program development, and evaluation, and flipped what we learned to make it relevant to Unity. I've also created sections that highlight lessons learned through discovery and reflection. These sections are entitled "Flipping Leadership," "Flipping Operations," and "Flipping" any other functional area of building an organization. These lessons are a direct parallel between how we innovate and flip ideas in hip hop.

One last thing. If you'd like to dig deeper into building tangible processes around your social impact ideas, you can access tools and resources at epicleadership.ca/bookresources.

SPARK
Hip Hop + Mental Health

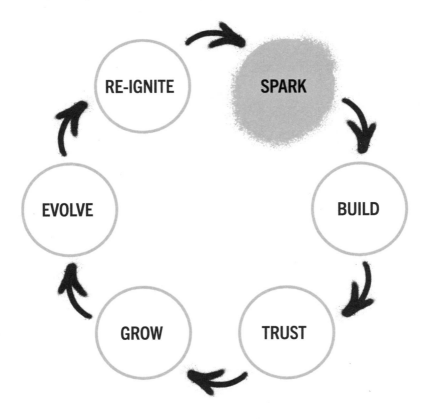

We all have our own coming-of-age story, and for me many of the lessons that turned out to be the best felt horrible at the time. These were moments that challenged me to my core. I wouldn't be who I am if I hadn't experienced those life-defining moments that challenged me to bounce back — and felt the pain that often came with them — and, on the flip side, those moments I got to celebrate unimaginable wins.

Throughout the book, you will meet different families. I'd like to start the book with the family I was born into.

MOMMA G

In breakin' you are given an alias, often defined by your crew or those who know you best. Like an alter ego. When I was younger, I gave my mom her b-girl name, her a.k.a.: I called her Momma Goose. This eventually evolved into Momma G because, for lack of a better explanation, she is a "G."

Over the course of my life, on my path to building Unity, I've been moulded not only by my experiences, but also by people — specifically, my parents. My mom gave — and continues to give — me hope. She instilled courage and resilience in me, and I often reflect on how it is her strength that gives me strength when I need it most. She is my guardian angel. I am so proud to see her living and loving life after everything she has endured. She is my rock of support, even though she may not always see it.

When I was six years old, my dad drove my mom to the emergency room in the middle of the night. I remember my dad telling me that my mom was sick. I learned she had a mental illness called schizophrenia. I didn't cry. I was stunned. I held my silence deep in my chest, where it lay dormant like a cat in the night, tucked into a place of refuge in an alleyway.

I remember my dad telling me that my mom was sick. I learned she had a mental illness called schizophrenia. We visited her in the hospital, and it was scary and confusing. I loved my mom so much, and I didn't know what this all meant at the time. My mom often tells me that she wouldn't wish a mental illness on her worst enemy. At the darkest times, my mom told me that my brother and I were the only things keeping up her will to live when she was in and out of the hospital, as doctors tried to find the right balance of medications to keep her stable. My Bubby, my mom's mom, always told her, "You gotta get better! You have two boys who need you." This experience pushed me to mature at a young age so I could be there for my mom.

When my mom would stop eating, I knew things were taking a turn for the worse. She thought her food was being poisoned; this was a sign her schizophrenia was taking over. She thought people were trying to hurt us or steal from us. She heard voices. Every time her medications were changed in an attempt to find the right balance, to keep her stable, Mom would have another breakdown, and we would need to take her to the hospital. Visiting my mom in the hospital was always scary.

I remember walking through a poorly lit hospital hallway and down a long staircase to a corridor with a locked door. The air was stale and cold. The door buzzed, and we stepped through. We had to check in at security. I didn't feel welcome. I heard someone screaming as we walked through the hallways. I wanted to cry but held it in. I was a quiet kid, but there was a lot I wanted to say. I felt a kind of pressure or constriction in my throat, a feeling I got used to.

I remember seeing my mom sitting on a bench in the hallway between several rooms that looked like prison cells. We sat there together and didn't say much. I knew something was wrong, but I didn't understand what. My mom embraced me tightly. I told her I loved her. I felt safe in her arms. We cried in silence. Our shirts stained with tears, we walked around the facility. I was startled by an older lady in a hospital gown shouting in a room with a ping-pong table. My mom showed us her room and then walked some more. As we passed by the central hub with a glass window, the nurses watched us. It wasn't a long visit, but it is one I'll never forget. My mom taught me the power of a good hug.

When we left my mom at the hospital that day, I felt like I was leaving a part of myself behind. I felt confused, sad, and empty, but I kept my feelings to myself.

After my parents divorced, in 2003, I moved back and forth between my mom and dad every three days, alternating Sundays. Soon after the divorce, mom had one final breakdown. I remember going to the hospital alone after school to visit when I was in high school. I bottled up my stress in a pressure chamber of silence. It was so bad, my stomach ached. I would have done anything to help her get better.

Mom's doctor finally found the right balance of meds that enabled her to stay stable, and she hasn't had a breakdown since I was a teenager.

My mom lives a happy life, even after all she has endured, filled with dancing, painting, and spending time with family. Her psychiatrist told her, "It's because of people like you that I come to work every day. Not everyone with schizophrenia gets better. God gave you a second chance in life."

I see my mom as a warrior of light and love. She always tells me she thinks guardian angels watched over her when she was sick. She is my guardian angel.

I love to see Momma G experience joy after everything she's been through. When she remarried, I danced with her at the wedding. I cried uncontrollable tears of joy on her shoulder as we moved in rhythm, celebrating the rollercoaster that is life. She told me she was happy. The contrast between that moment and the struggle she endured brought about in me a deep and profound appreciation: All those hospital visits, breakdowns, surviving breast cancer, and now this moment. I knew then, as I know now, I will never forget this dance.

Several years later, her husband tragically and suddenly passed away. He was so kind to my mother — he was kind to everyone, and honest and hard working — I couldn't thank him enough for being there for her. His passing brought another very difficult time. Our family was becoming familiar with tragedy, but that's not how my mom experienced life. She enjoyed the life she had, even as these events put things into new forms of perspective. She was always focused on the simple yet profound elements: family, dancing, hugs. I worried that the stress of my stepdad's passing might lead my mom to another mental health breakdown, but somehow, she stood strong. To this day, she pursues her hobbies and fills her time with painting and dancing. She orders a large double-double at Tim Hortons every day.

After many years of ups and downs, she has built a new life. She has a new boyfriend, and every day of the week she is either going out dancing, going to a street festival, or drinking white wine at some karaoke bar. These days, she goes out later and more often than I do!

> Whenever I'm deeply struggling, I ask myself, "How would Momma G deal with this?" This reflection has helped me through some of the toughest times. To me, Momma G is an embodiment of hope, strength, and resilience.

PAPA PIECEZ

My dad has always been proud of me. He always told me as a kid, "When I grow up, I want to be just like you." My dad's ongoing battle with Parkinson's disease affected our entire family. Parkinson's is a progressive illness, meaning there is never a road back to health. There is no cure. Throughout my twenties, my dad's Parkinsons started getting worse a lot faster and I began to lose the father I knew growing up.

My dad is everyone's favourite person. He's my favourite person, too, next to Mom. He's everyone's mentor. He's my mentor. He is the centre of all social circles he's part of. But Parkinson's has slowly begun to change this. Parkinson's causes him to freeze up and limits his ability to move and walk. But this wasn't what changed things. Where things really took a turn for the worse was when he lost his drive, his will. He began to give up. How could the strongest person I know give up? I'd have never thought it'd happen, but I was seeing him lose hope more and more every few weeks.

In 2015, my dad learned about an incredible and relatively new surgery called deep brain stimulation (DBS), where doctors implant an electric-shock device (almost like a pacemaker for the brain). When successful, this surgery can increase a person's ability to function dramatically, but the effectiveness varies from patient to patient. Although there is still no cure for Parkinson's, this surgery could improve my dad's quality of life. But like any brain surgery, it has its risks. Dad underwent several tests to see if he qualified for the surgery. We got the great news that he qualified, and a date was set for the surgery. Before his operation, I remember him saying, "Follow your passion and do what you love, no matter what." He always said this to me, but this time it sunk to my core. When he came out of surgery, the doctors said the operation was a success, and that he would get a lot of his function back.

A few weeks passed, and my dad began to heal, but we noticed there was yellow pus coming from his incision. The doctor gave him antibiotics and told him to stop scratching.

At 2:45 one morning, my phone began to buzz on the table next to my bed. I looked at the screen. It was Katherine, my stepmom, calling. She told me that my dad needed to be rushed to the hospital.

Mel, my fiancée, and I drove immediately to the hospital, which was only five minutes away. We arrived before the ambulance. I was there to see him as the ambulance came around the corner and pulled up to the emergency doors. As I stood beside the gurney and held his hand, he had a seizure. I thought he was dying right there and then, and I was going to see it happen.

What the hell happened? I'd thought the surgery was a success. We waited for hours before the doctor told us that Dad was having seizures and they were looking into the cause. They found an infection in his brain. His surgery was the one in a thousand that goes wrong. After seeing him have that seizure, all I could think was the worst, replaying it in my head again and again.

Day to day, we weren't sure if he would make it. After over two weeks in the hospital, my dad began losing hope, and there were some really dark days. I couldn't believe the outpouring of support from thousands (yes, thousands) of people. It was truly overwhelming. It was so overwhelming that we created a website to give updates. People could also post comments there, and I could read them to my dad, so he didn't have to expend his strength on a lot of visitors. My dad needed to rest.

After many months, his brain infection slowly healed, his condition stabilized, and he was finally sent home. The next few months, he recovered at a snail's pace. I got my dad back and he slowly began to get back his drive for life.

He got a second chance in life, and I appreciate every day we have with him.

My dad always told me before every b-boy battle I entered as a teenager, "It doesn't matter if you win or lose, as long as you win." I would then go on to win every one of those battles. I won over twenty battles with him by my side. Dad would sneak me into clubs when I was only fourteen, the grimiest venues such as the Comfort Zone in Toronto, where my dance mentor Benzo used to throw local breakin' jams.

> My dad always supported me, telling me to follow my passion, no matter what. He even became a father figure to many dancers in the breakin' scene because their parents often weren't present. People would call him "B-Boy Daddio" and "Papa Piecez." Sometimes it's easier to have never had something than to have something great and lose it suddenly.

CIRCUS DREAMS AND FUSED VERTEBRAE

I was a quiet kid growing up. I didn't speak about my troubles with friends or family, often bottling up what I really wanted to say. I figure that's why dance became my voice, my outlet, my alter ego.

When I was young, I loved climbing the cabinets and walls in my house. Anything I could get a grip on I would attach myself to, and my mom would yell at me to stop. I'm still not sure whether I did it because I liked climbing or because I wanted to get my mom's attention. Eventually I began standing on my head in front of the TV. I would watch cartoons for hours as my face turned red as a cherry. This concerned my mom so much that she enrolled me in a gymnastics class so I wouldn't break my neck. I was only five years old at the time.

For a while, I loved gymnastics; it was one of the few places I felt truly free. Eventually my gymnastics instructor saw I was getting good, and to help get me competition ready, he would push me all the way down in the splits and sit on my back. I quit gymnastics when I was ten years old because it stopped being fun. But I took away something that changed my life forever — the ability to walk on my hands.

I loved being upside down. I became obsessed with it. Soon I began to walk around my house on my hands, creating challenges and games for myself, setting up upside-down obstacle courses. I learned to walk in circles, learned to balance on one hand. I even flipped light switches with my toes while inverted. Eventually I built up the courage to walk down the stairs on my hands. One day, as I was walking around upstairs on my hands, I passed near the top of the staircase. My mom yelled at me to be careful, but I decided this was the perfect moment — while I had her attention — to try to take the stairs upside down. My first downstairs handstand walk was accompanied by a soundtrack of my mom screaming at me: my motivation to not fail. I made it to the bottom without losing my balance. Soon after, I challenged myself to walk up the stairs on my hands. This was significantly more difficult and took a lot longer to figure out.

I created endless games to push my limits and increase my balance and strength upside down. This proved to be useful when I started b-boying around the time I was thirteen years old. By this age, I had already developed the body control and core strength needed to move in nearly any way my mind could dream up. Every time I saw a new move, I needed to learn it, and I was able to learn almost every move I saw within one to two weeks. I became obsessed with expanding my dance vocabulary and pushing my limits. I eventually began combining moves in different and unlikely sequences creating new possibilities. This despite my grade two teacher, Ms. Yetman, having told my mom that there was something wrong with my neck. I couldn't turn my head. But life continued on.

When I was in grade twelve, applying to go to university for business, I also auditioned for Cirque du Soleil. After a gruelling and strange audition process that lasted two long days, I made it. I remember a moment in the audition where the artistic director asked me to do a freestyle dance solo — in slow motion with my shirt off — to pop rock music from the 1970s. I think they wanted to see if I would be willing to step out of my comfort zone (and ultimately do whatever they asked). That was far from comfortable, but I gave it my best. A room full of thirty dancers got cut down to five. I made it into the pool of performers for Cirque du Soleil. I also got acceptance letters from Ryerson and York universities. This was a pivotal moment in my life. I could literally run away to Las Vegas and join the circus or go to school. I went back and forth on this decision for months. Finally, I chose to go to school to pursue doing something bigger for others instead of selfishly pursuing my dream to dance. I knew I was bound for bigger things, not just for myself.

When I was sixteen years old, I started feeling pain and tingling in my body after doing too many slow headspins. I guess my grade two teacher was right. I got worried and scheduled an appointment for an MRI, which took place several months later. I learned some troubling news: I had three naturally fused vertebrae — C_4, C_5, and C_6 — in my neck. This condition severely limited my ability to rotate my head and caused soreness, but that became the least of my concerns.

When I met a neurologist, he told me that this condition put my future mobility at risk, and I might face paralysis or even death. He told me, having seen my MRI, he was shocked that I didn't have constant headaches or chronic pain.

There is supposed to be cartilage between each vertebra that allows for mobility and flexibility around the nerves and spinal cord. My fused vertebrae had no cartilage and no space between them. Most major nerves flow through the neck to the rest of the body. If a nerve became pinched between vertebrae, I could lose feeling in my arms, legs, or entire body. The likelihood of this happening increased if I participated in extreme physical activity.

The doctor told me a story of a young patient he had who also had naturally fused neck vertebrae. He told me he was a very active basketball player who refused to stop playing. One day during a game, his disc slipped, resulting in paralysis from the neck down. I was born with this condition, but apparently spinning on my head, particularly in slow motion, wasn't helping.

Not wanting to think about what could be worse than being paralyzed, I stopped dancing.

I really thought my dance career was over until I met Luca "Lazylegz" Patuelli, a b-boy who dances and lives life to the fullest with a condition called arthrogryposis. He can barely walk because of limited muscle growth in his legs, yet he uses crutches to assist his dancing and focus on his strengths. His message of "No Excuses, No Limits" resonated with me right away. He is one of my best friends and biggest inspirations. He inspired me to reinvent my dancing without touching my head to the floor. I soon had a comeback and won an international battle in Holland in 2011 after thinking it was all done. I flipped my style and created a new way of moving my body that wouldn't likely injure me permanently. I also found Ashley Gilbert, a massage therapist who literally worked magic on my neck, giving me neck mobility I never could have dreamed of. In short, I got an education, stopped spinning on my head, and learned to live with a chronic neck condition. I remember my Grampa always said, "You need to dance the way the music plays. If life plays a waltz, you don't dance the foxtrot." I learned to adapt to challenges instead of giving up.

FINDING MY VOICE THROUGH BREAKIN'

For readers unfamiliar with b-boying or breakin', it is often incorrectly referred to as break dancing. When it blew up in the media, people started calling the style *break dance* because it was easier for the public to understand. In order to be respectful of hip hop culture, we try never to use the term "break dance."

When I saw b-boying for the first time, I was an awkward teenager attending a bar mitzvah. I saw one of the most famous b-boy crews in Canada, the Boogie Brats, throw down. A dancer named Mighty Mouse did a handstand and spun, three times on one hand. With all the shit going on in my life at the time, seeing this gave me peace for just a few brief moments. I knew I needed it. I went home that night and searched online for "break dancing." This was before the advent of Google and YouTube, so nothing really came up except one hit, breakdance.com, which was a website that had explanations of moves in text. Video wasn't a thing on the internet at that time, given the speed of dial-up modems.

It was nearly impossible to translate breakin' from text, but I did everything I could to learn via this incomprehensible format. My dad always encouraged me to follow my passion, and as soon as he saw me dancing at home he looked around for classes. He stumbled upon a class every Saturday at Randolph Academy for the Performing Arts in downtown Toronto. We went up to the third floor in a shaky elevator, and I was so excited to finally learn to break from someone who really knew what they were doing. Benzo, from world-famous Canadian breakin' crew Bag of Trix, was one of the best teachers in Canada. Benzo took me under his wing, and the rest is history. Everything he taught me, I'd learn within a week. He snuck my dad and me into battles at bars and took me to parties and practice sessions. It was my intro to hip hop culture. At first, I was worried because I was the only white, Jewish b-boy on the scene. Once I proved myself on the dance floor, though, people began to accept me for who I was. I gave respect where it was due, a fundamental value in hip hop, and received respect in return. I will never forget when Benzo brought me to my first performance when I was thirteen. My dad hung with us backstage. Benzo, Tony, and I danced alongside Maestro Fresh Wes at Nathan Phillips Square on New Year's Eve with a sea of people. After throwing down a clean headspin at the edge of the runway surrounded by the crowd, Maestro pulled me over, put his arm around my shoulder and we waved our hand back and forth to a seemingly endless crowd. All the stress in my life melted away for a moment. Hip hop made me feel like I was part of something larger than life itself; I felt valued for who I was and what I had to contribute.

A few years later, when I was fifteen, I met a few members of Maximum Efficiency Crew (MEC) at Benzo's class — John and Floorplay — who invited me to practice at Secord Community Centre. After a few sessions, they battled me into the crew, which became my second family. My b-boy journey transformed beyond being just an outlet; it became my community. I was one of the youngest kids on the scene, going to clubs and battles, so people started to call me Little Mikey. In fact, Mighty Mouse, the legendary Boogie Brats b-boy I saw at the bar mitzvah, was the one who gave me this name. Later, my crew gave me my breakin' name Piecez, because my style was powerful and I loved stacking freezes like a well-known breaker from Style Elements Crew in L.A. named Crumbs. My crew told me, "You are either going to be 'Piecez' or 'Chunks,' because it sounds like 'Crumbs.'" I chose Piecez.

B-boying gave me an outlet for dealing with my anxiety and bottled-up anger. It gave me an escape from what was going on at home and became my creative jet fuel. I felt accepted and valued for who I was on the dance floor. I found my community, my alter ego. I created a different persona on the dance floor. I became connected to something bigger than me. Hip hop was a vast community that I was just beginning to get exposed to. I explored new parts of myself that I didn't bring out on a daily basis with family or friends at school. Breakin' for me was like putting on a superhero costume, and new things became possible even though underneath the mask and persona I was still the same person. Hip hop gave me courage. My life was transformed; I could define myself based on my contribution, not where I came from. This led me to wanting to share this gift with others.

THE POWER OF COMMUNITY

Beyond dancing, the b-boying community is a powerful one that has truly taken me in, as it does with anyone who is part of its beautiful culture. It's a common rule in breakin' that if a b-boy or b-girl is in your city, you need to take care of them because you know the favour will always be returned. If you're a b-boy or b-girl, you always have a couch to sleep on, no matter where you are. The dance is amazing, but the community is honestly the best part of hip hop culture: It makes me feel like I have a family anywhere I go in the world. It's like a secret society that you can only prove you're part of based on your skill, how you dress, and even how you carry yourself. You can even identify a b-boy based on how they shake your hand.

One night in Tokyo, I went to the local practice spot at Mizonokuchi Station. The dancers practice in the subway station because the floor is smooth and there is a lot of space. Someone on an online dance forum mentioned this local practice spot, so I thought I would check it out. The only issue was the practice started at 11:00 p.m., and the trains stopped running at midnight. This station was almost two hours away from my hostel, so I would have no way of getting back. I chanced it and went to check it out. I figured someone would take me in.

When I got there, the level of talent was incredible. Some of the best dancers in Japan were there that night: B-Boy Katsu, Taisuke, and the All Area Crew. Each circle has its unsaid rank. When I arrived, there were three distinct circles where people were practising. The beginners practised in one circle, intermediate-to-advanced in another, and the OGs in another. I immediately jumped into the most experienced cypher and got battled as soon as I stepped in. I hit my set clean and proved my place in the pecking order. I began talking with Katsu, one of the leaders of All Area Crew who ran the session. He was a super cool guy.

By the end of the session, I was drenched in sweat from the humidity and covered in dirt from the subway floor. I stank. By this point it was 2:00 a.m. I had no way of getting to my hostel, so I planned to just chill in the station until it opened again at 6:00 a.m. Katsu told me not to be crazy and to come stay at his apartment. I went over to his spot and we hung out all night. When chilling in his apartment, he said, "Wait a second, I know you! Are you that b-boy who was in the UK B-Boy Championships 2004 one-on-one battle?" He popped the tape into his VCR, and we watched my battle against Omar from Jive Turkeys. I couldn't believe this guy in Japan who I had just met and looked up to actually knew who I was. We joked around all night and eventually I crashed on his couch. We've been good friends ever since. Before he dropped me off at the subway station, he gave me one of his crew shirts to keep as an extended member of the All Area Crew family. I gave him a Unity shirt, and we parted ways.

This has happened to me more times than I can count. Similar but different b-boy and b-girl connections have happened for me in the USA, China, Taiwan, Spain, Sweden, the Netherlands, Jamaica, Italy, and several other places around the world. Sometimes I wish people treated each other with this type of unconditional respect outside of the breakin' scene, but the fact is the commonality of the dance and the culture that surrounds it is a magnetic force that brings us together like nothing else. It is what real community feels like. A common community all over the world. A b-boy I met in Hong Kong said it best: "Every day everybody is your brother." I wanted to share this community through Unity's work and create a movement that shared hip hop with those who resonated with its principles of peace, love, unity, and having fun, as broadcast in the song by Afrika Bambaataa and James Brown.

"EXPRESS YOUR STRESS"

Like I said, I was a quiet kid. Even to this day, when I'm angry, I want to beat up the floor. Stress provides a creative opportunity for me: it fuels my dance. The biggest challenges in my life have given rise to new angles and perspectives to fuel my creativity. It's when I have the most to share, something to say, but words can't express the story. It's the raw expression birthed from experiences translated through movement. I express, create, and heal in order to better understand and communicate my experiences. I turn pain into power.

In 2003, I had an idea. I wanted to share hip hop as a tool to create social change. Hip hop was such a powerful instrument in my life. It was an expression, an outlet, a voice, a platform, a community. In grade eleven, as part of a group project in my entrepreneurship class, our teacher, Mr. Izumi, gave us a practical real-world assignment. We had to write a business plan for an entrepreneurial venture that we would have to execute to raise money for a local charity of our choice. Our group ran an event we called "Hip Hop Away From Violence." We donated the proceeds from the event to the charity Leave Out ViolencE (LOVE), a charity that works with youth in underserved communities, providing them outlets and alternatives to violence through photojournalism.

The first event was a miserable failure. Everything that could go wrong went wrong. We needed to sell enough tickets to fill the school gym, which held up to four hundred students. A few days before the event, we had only sold around thirty tickets. We decided to move to a smaller venue. The only venue we could get permission from the principal to use at the last minute was the cafeteria during lunch hour. This changed the entire dynamic of the event. It was terrible. No one paid attention. All the performers felt disrespected. Luckily, the charity we were working with cancelled their guest speaker, because it would have been an embarrassment. On top of everything else, a few of our best performers dropped out. We went through the motions and ran the event the best we could, but it was a disaster. I knew we could do better. We had to give it another shot. I still believed.

In grade twelve, I was elected president of the student council and decided our big event that year would be Hip Hop Away From Violence. This time, we started preparing almost six months before the event date, getting students engaged in both planning and selling tickets. We also secured a much stronger roster of performers to headline the show. In the end, we ended up selling over three hundred tickets and raised a bunch of money for LOVE. Over three hundred of my peers respect-fully listened to real stories of youth who had experienced violence. We had engaged a room full of young people with a message that was truly important, using hip hop as the hook. It was youth led and youth driven. We were onto something.

I decided to continue this work. When I went on to York University, I helped found a student club we called "LOVE at York." I sat on the board of directors of LOVE in Toronto. At first, they allowed Hip Hop Away From Violence to operate as one of their programs. Once we began expanding to more schools, they told us we needed to separate from their organization. I think LOVE's board began to see us as a liability as we grew. We broke off, took our programs, and registered as a student club at York. I remember sitting in our office in the student centre, brainstorming new names for our club with Amy Forristal, who was an engaged volunteer and artist in our early days. Amy said, "What about Unity?" Everything we did brought people together through hip hop. It was Unity. It was perfect. Unity was born. Our tagline was "Express your stress and develop skills for success."

When I graduated from York, I decided I wanted to carry on, and at the time of publication of this book Unity is still going strong. After fifteen years, Unity has had an impact on over a quarter of a million youth across Canada; it had thirteen full-time staff, four part-time staff, eighty artist educators on contract, thirty-one community partnerships, forty-eight major funders, and 184 donors. One of the core philosophies of hip hop culture is that it provides a platform to create something out of nothing. We applied this mentality and built a movement.

There was a lot I loved about building Unity, but there was also a lot that really killed me inside. I will try to be as honest as I can about both. My hope is to provide a realistic picture of what it took for our team to build a sustainable organization that could move forward without its founder. It may help to put into perspective that everything naturally comes to an end and great things can continue without the person who started them.

I trusted in the idea behind using hip hop to make

a positive change in the world. It took sweat, tears, and many tiny steps to bring our dream to reality.

I will share things that I learned and philosophies about breakin' that I incorporated into my leadership and management style. I encourage anyone with an idea or spark to build something that will make a positive impact in your community, and to do it in your own way.

SPARK REFLECTION QUESTIONS

1. What motivates you to make a positive and responsible impact in your community?
2. What does *responsible* impact mean to you?
3. What experiences and goals in your life spark your drive to create change?
4. How can you better understand where your drive comes from and what more you can learn from your spark?
5. How do you know there is a need for your change-making idea? What proof of this can you gather?
6. What assumptions do you have around your change-making idea? How can you test each of your assumptions?
7. What good intentions do you have that you need to challenge?
8. What more do you need to learn before taking your idea to the next step and testing it?
9. What support networks do you have currently? What creative ways can you build new networks of support?
10. Do you have a mentor? Who can you ask to mentor you within your current network? What creative ways can you find mentors outside of your network?

BUILD
Building the Plane While Flying It

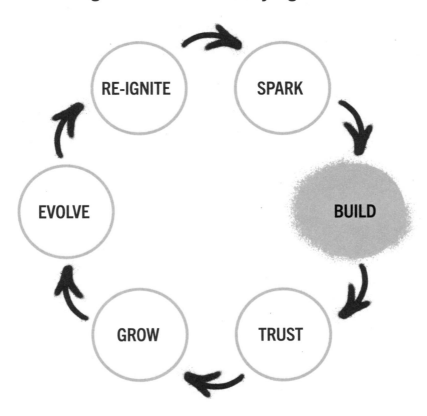

My hands are shaking. I'm tearing up. I can barely speak. I'm frozen.

It feels like my chest is going to jump out of my throat.

Although I'm in no real danger, nothing has ever felt more real than the terror going through my veins.

This is anxiety. Real deal anxiety.

I take a deep breath and keep moving forward.

I go to my next meeting, do my next presentation, go on with my day as normal. But I don't feel well.

I've decided:

I'm not going to let this own my life.

I will not let it win.

I can live a great life, even if I feel terrible inside.

I owe it to myself and everyone around me to continue moving forward despite how I feel.

This experience is the most perplexing challenge I have ever faced.

When I'm in control I can handle it.

A hundred emails a day? No problem!

Twelve meetings a day with no breaks in four locations across the city? No problem!

Eating while doing a phone conference while driving to a program in Mississauga with someone in my car? No problem!

Until it is a problem, and now I've learned, a problem I can't change.

Or is it a problem? Am I a problem? NO.

I am me. With every great thing and every not so great thing in me.

I will continue to always be me despite my anxiety, my illness.

Is it an illness? Or more of a challenge?

I am not my anxiety.

I am a person who cares and loves and gives everything I can.

I am a b-boy who dances to feel and express my story.

I am not the sleepless nights or the panic attacks.

I am not my anxiety.

Although it is scary, I will not live in fear.

I will live with pride, joy, self-worth.

Feelings everyone deserves.

Although it's as real as rain, it is distorted pain.

If I can recognize this with no intention to change it, I do not become it.

I get to be me, with it.

It's a moon-cast shadow in my day, but the clouds always clear even if there is a hurricane, a typhoon, or tornado.

It feels like the end, but it is not.

It is part of the journey, my new path.

It's part of me, my day, my life.

I won't resist or avoid.

I will just be with my anxiety.

On a Valentine's Day evening in a dimly lit Toronto restaurant with hipster décor, I sat with my beautiful fiancée, Mel, to unwind and enjoy a night together after what seemed like a relatively busy but typical week. But as soon as we sat down, I felt something wasn't right. My hands were sweaty, and my heart was beating in my throat. I felt like my insides were trying to jump out of my body. The waiter came around to ask for our drinks order, and I couldn't even speak. I began to shake. Mel asked me what was wrong, and I tried to answer, but I couldn't. I felt tears welling up in my eyes. The intensity grew and then fear kicked in. I felt genuine panic. Mel asked me again what was wrong. I began to cry hysterically.

When my first anxiety attack happened, I didn't know what was happening to me or why. This became part of the anxiety — the fear of not understanding my reaction. I thought I was losing my mind. With a mother with a history of mental illness, worst-case scenarios overtook my thoughts. I needed to try to figure out what was happening to me. I needed to solve this.

I went to my family doctor and then eventually to a therapist. I began to reflect on my past stress. My mind took me back to high school. I had joined the student council, as I'd felt I needed to do something beyond the usual classroom stuff. Every year there was an event where the high school bands would play at a show called *SWAY*. This particular year, the show was a bit of a disaster, and the person who was supposed to be leading it left others to pick up the broken pieces of the event and run with it. In addition to putting out fires, I got assigned to door duty because there was a "door issue." Someone had sold tickets to students who attended other schools, and our show was supposed to be restricted to students from our school. So, I was given the job of telling people who had bought tickets they couldn't see the show if they didn't have a student card.

Our principal, Mr. Selby, stood by the front door, hanging over my shoulder to make sure I didn't let in anyone who wasn't a student at our school. To top it off, I had also been given contradictory instructions from the student council president to let all his friends in. I was trapped in the middle of something that wasn't going to end well. My stomach churned at the thought of disappointing everyone. There was no winning here. Anything I did would piss off someone. It was one of the first times I realized that I hated dealing with conflict.

I remember trying to make small talk with Mr. Selby and realizing I couldn't breathe properly. What the hell was going on? I went to the washroom, not wanting attention from the principal. My hands went cold, my heart raced, my breathing sped up drastically. I couldn't catch my breath, so I tried breathing faster and faster, but it wasn't working.

I went back to take care of the door situation. After about five minutes of trying to ignore whatever was happening in my body, I fell over. My hand contracted towards my chest. I thought I was having a heart attack. The fear snowballed into a complete state of panic. Next thing I knew, an ambulance was at my school and I was on a stretcher. My hand began to seize up uncontrollably. I thought I was dying. The paramedic told me to slow down my breathing. For some reason, I thought I needed to breathe faster. The paramedic whipped out a brown paper bag and said, "Breathe into this." Gradually, I stopped hyperventilating.

For the rest of my time in high school, I carried a brown paper bag in my knapsack to stop me from hyperventilating. Initially it happened about once a week, and then it tapered off to once a month, and eventually it stopped altogether.

I remember at future events when I'd feel the same loss of breath coming on, I would lock myself in the student council office and whip out my paper bag, ensuring first that no one was around to see. I missed many days of school because my stomach was terribly affected by the stress I bottled up from all the issues at home and from overworking myself in every aspect of my life.

I avoided facing what was going on at home by filling my time by working extra hard. When something was wrong in my life, I suppressed it by pushing the pedal to the metal on everything else. I filled my time with doing anything but addressing the issue. I got involved in student clubs, played a ton of video games, and went deep into dancing to fill the gaps. These were my escapes from reality.

I struggled in school. Most concepts like essay writing, reading, and math that my peers seemed to breeze through took me weeks to get a handle on. I hid my struggles until they could no longer be avoided. In grade six, I got a tutor who taught me how to read, because I had managed to get by pretending to read until then. My anxiety in school was so high that I dodged classes. I told my teachers I had stomach aches, which eventually began to manifest physically from internal stress. (I later learned that avoidance is one of the key elements that reinforces anxiety by enabling it.) The more I applied myself to keep up my grades, the more I was stressed to the limit. And my stress was amplified by what was going on at home with my mom in and out of the hospital and the fallout from my folks' divorce.

Dance was my outlet, my community. It allowed me to express my stress and give voice to all of the anger and buried emotion that was flowing through my veins. But my anxiety attacks were not done.

Breakin' and Building: There Are No Shortcuts — Just Practice and Perseverance

I like to create by bringing together unlikely people, places, and things. Some of my most incredible and unobvious creations have come from a process I call *finding B*. Let me break it down. I know how to do two separate breakin' moves, a backspin and a handstand — let's call them *A* and *C*. Let's assume I've never tried to combine these two moves together before to get from backspin up to a handstand, but can do each move individually. In order to get from *A* to *C*, I need to figure out what to do in the middle to get from my back to my hands without touching my feet. This is *B*. Let the pain begin.

What is *B*? Instead of asking myself questions or writing things down on a piece of paper to try to figure it out, I just visualize *A*, I visualize *C*, then I attempt to fill in the blank and solve for *B*. I am aware of my strengths, and based on this I attempt to combine movements that have never been put together. This doesn't always work. Sometimes I can try the same combination for years before I figure out *B*. But after attempting *A* to *C* again and again, I become stronger, more flexible, and I increase my muscle memory. Eventually, after many hours of practice, I find *B*. Backspin to handstand. Now that combination becomes *A*, and I can add it to a series of longer combinations I've developed. This directly parallels how I develop and test ideas in building an organization.

Freestyling is a major part of breakin', and one of my favourite parts. It is improvising movement based on what the music is telling me and where the movement of a given situation is taking me. It's a split-second decision and reaction to everything that is happening around me. I choose a new direction based on where I am, without any forethought. It has taught me to listen and respond to the moment, to be in the present. The ability to freestyle has parallels in many aspects of my life as it teaches me to work with what I have with serious time constraints (i.e., gravity doesn't wait when you're freestyling, and it sure isn't forgiving if you don't react in time).

The beauty is I am always leveling up, building off the foundations I learned and developed earlier. Slowly, over time, with consistency and hard work, I can do anything. As I become able to do one new "impossible" thing, I then attempt to connect it to another "impossible" thing, thereby creating a brand-new thing I never before thought possible. It's all about the process and the work put in.

I don't waste time when I practice. I try to be efficient. When I go to an open session, I see some dancers literally sit around for three hours talking shit and only throw down a few times. But I make the most out of every minute. I say hi to everyone quickly, warm up, stretch, and go *all out*. By the end of every session, I'm drenched in sweat and have had a full-body workout usually within an hour. With this mentality, I accomplish more in one hour than some dancers do in three. I am always looking for ways to be efficient when training and learning. Maybe that's why our crew is called Maximum *Efficiency* Crew.

I quickly discovered that there are no shortcuts to B. There is nothing I could tell someone, no formula, no tricks — it was just practice. *Finding B* is simply practice. The more I practised, the more I could create new "impossible" combinations and moves based on what I was comfortable with as I continued to level up. I could literally feel my comfort zone expanding.

What was hard for me five years ago is simple for me today. It's become part of my comfort zone. I know this may sound like the obvious progression towards developing any talent or skill. However, the discipline to repeat something that wasn't working until it works was what made me able to do things that people look at and say "Holy shit." Sometimes even I watch things I've done and say "Holy shit." I love doing things where I can surprise myself.

This is the same mindset I used to build Unity, and it served me well through all its ups and downs. I didn't have a concrete plan, but I had a direction. I wasn't afraid to get down and do the hard work it would take for Unity to succeed.

In breakin', *biting* is what we say when someone copies a move, or way of moving, from another dancer. It's highly frowned upon. Rather than copying, you can *flip* ideas: Learn to make them your own by adding your unique style, creating something new from a foundation learned previously. Combine new ideas that have never been put together to create something that no one has ever done. This is the beauty in the creation process of breakin' — building based on strengths and a foundation learned from others in the community.

Sometimes I don't even know what my destination is when I'm dancing, what *C* is, I just know where I'm starting. I throw myself in a direction that I'm relatively familiar with (or not) with a lot of force and at a new angle and see what happens. I take a risk. This to me is the essence of combining adrenaline with experience, I often execute a move that I know I will never do again. I often record my dancing on video, then review the footage to teach myself what I did spontaneously. This may sound ridiculous, but sometimes I cannot imagine creating something that happens naturally in the moment. So, I create situations where I can be "in the moment," but record it. I later watch these videos of my honest and true expression and bite the best parts.

I was able to apply this approach directly to experimentation and my own growing self-reflection when building Unity: I created experimental playgrounds, recreating certain "moments" in breakin' that I later rewatched and copied. For example, I would try to recreate the final round of a long battle. To do this I would do several minutes of continuous six steps until I was completely exhausted. Then I'd take a ten-second break and throw down my hardest set and film it. I think to myself, "Perform like you're in the finals of the biggest battle of your life." This inspires the feeling of the final round of an important battle. The moment of truth. It tests my stamina, strength, and mindset when I am the most tired but know I need to pull through and kill that one final set to win one for the team.

Another way I bite myself is through visualizing a combo that I've dreamed up but never been able to put together in real life. I'll dance intensely for five minutes nonstop, until I'm completely out of breath and my heart rate is high. Once the adrenaline is flowing through my body, I catch my breath and then blast my favourite music, usually anything produced by J Dilla — RIP to the Detroit legend — and I bring visualizations to the floor in real time. No hesitating. The only rule is *don't stop*: keep moving even if I crash. It all happens lightning fast. When I rewatch these videos later, I pick out the good parts and bite my own "in the moment" combos and moves. Biting myself in this way is a safe playground for experimentation and innovation.

Self-awareness is critical to executing when I don't have time to think about every little thing. I'm still aware of my body and how I feel to avoid injury. Biting myself has allowed me to really look inward to explore my strengths and reflect on where I want to improve. This reflection was foundational to building Unity.

Breakin' New Ground: Originality and Innovation

I started Unity as a fifteen-year-old. I had no formal leadership experience. I wasn't naïve to the fact that I needed to learn a lot. It was like sprinting constantly in an endless race. There was no finish line, always another task, to-do, or new idea to launch. I worked relentlessly because I believed the idea of using hip hop to improve young people's lives was worth investing my time in. It had done that very thing in my own life and in the lives of many of my friends in the hip hop community. I knew this was going to work, but I didn't know how. My next "battle" had begun. How do I make this idea real? Where do I even start?

I live to make impossible things possible. Breakin' taught me that this was my mission in life. To me, impossible just means it hasn't been done yet. I often discover the most amazing new b-boy moves when I don't have a plan in mind, throwing myself in a direction with great force at a new angle to see what happens. Sometimes it's painful. I've fallen, smashed my head, neck, back, hips, shoulders, toes, fingers, and pretty much every body part imaginable (yes, every part). But I need to throw myself in dangerous positions, dive into uncharted territory, to discover new moves. Doing this also helps expose my weaknesses, uncovering areas where I need to work harder.

One of the hardest yet most rewarding things in my life is proving the impossible possible, right in front of people's eyes. For example, I really wanted to learn to balance on my head without my hands touching the floor. It seemed like an impossible feat, so I began the journey of learning how. After several weeks, I went from balancing for one second to three seconds to five seconds. But I couldn't balance for more than five seconds. I remember practising this move until I couldn't move my neck at all. I had to figure this out. I would not accept five seconds as my maximum. After repeating it thousands of times, I eventually figured out a trick. If I dropped my feet close to the ground and let my hip hang down, the move lowered my centre of gravity. When this happened, I had more leverage and space for balancing and controlling my ability to stay up longer. I also realized the skin on the top of my head had some flexibility, which gave me another leverage point for balance. All this combined, I eventually got up to ten seconds and then thirty, and finally I capped off around one minute. I did it. I pushed my limits to new levels.

So, I thought, what's next? Maybe, just maybe, I could spin in super slow motion! The new challenge meant serious pain. One of my teachers got concerned and asked my mom if something was wrong with my neck because I was stiff as a board in class. I carried on. After a few months I had figured it out. I could combine my no-hands head-balancing with slow spinning. I created the never-thought-possible slow-motion headspin.

On a good day, I could get about eight rotations in slow motion. I literally felt I was defying gravity. Although there was a logical sequence of training that brought me to that point, the result was unreal, even to me. It was the best feeling in the world. The only thing that topped that feeling was when people saw it for the first time. I would enter battles and drop my slow headspin to new crowds, who would literally lose their minds in disbelief.

I remember so many moments when the room just came down. It is the biggest rush I've ever felt in my life. I would do the first spin and people would start to clap, then the second slow spin and they'd begin hooting, the third spin you'd hear some hollers, by the fourth slow spin you would get people's "What the hell is happening?" reaction, and anything beyond that was just screaming, loud noises, and jumping around. Right in front of my eyes, they learned the earth was not flat and Santa Claus isn't real, and I was the one who pulled the rug from under their feet. To have an entire room of dancers in the community around me realizing something they'd never before seen done — something they would have deemed impossible only moments before they saw me do it — can actually happen is the most special thing. It was then I knew that my mission in life was to make the impossible possible.

Building a Plane While Flying It

In high school and to this day, I've had this relentless "get shit done" attitude and loved starting new projects. The problem was my drive had no brakes. This was both a gift and a curse. When it worked — growing and building a new idea into the world — it was very useful. On the other hand, when it involved me focusing on a worry that was not real or that I could not change, it would drive me into the ground or cause me to lose night after night of sleep. If I lost a night of sleep from worrying about something I couldn't control, I would often tell myself "I won't get through my important day tomorrow or be effective if I don't sleep," a story that would lead to yet another sleepless night in a vicious cycle. Instead of saying, "If I'm tired at my meeting, I'll do my best, be kind to myself, and likely no one will notice," I would be extra hard on myself. Piling judgments on top of what was happening only increased my anxiety. I needed to learn to ground my thoughts in reality to harness and balance this powerful drive inside of me.

Without a specific task or purpose to focus this energy on, I am a nervous wreck of uncontrollable spinning thoughts. B-boying helped me learn to manage my intense energy and give it direction and purpose.

I build a plane while flying it. I start with the foundation of an idea and immediately step off the metaphorical cliff to test it. It is the pressure of putting my ideas out in the real world when they aren't fully built that forces me to figure out the details. I have an intention that is strong and clear. Just as I do in breakin', I listen to my body and respond to the environment, I throw myself in a direction that feels right and figure out the details before I hit the ground. If I'm about to crash, I change course; if I'm soaring, I use momentum to enable new possibility. This was my approach to building Unity.

I love the intensity of the creation process in breakin'. Gravity is the time and space between one move and a face plant. It ups the ante; it's the force that pushes me into figuring out my next move based on the position I'm moving in and the direction in which I'm falling. All momentum can be used to transition into another move. I truly believe that *all momentum is good momentum*, even if it doesn't seem so. When I embody this idea, I become truly unstoppable through responsive adaptation. Even falling towards the ground quickly and at a seemingly dangerous, hopeless angle and speed. I make the choice to use my momentum to create something instead of crashing and hitting the floor. This combination of mind and body working together or against each other in a split second is called "crash and create." As I plummet to the floor, I have a choice to make: use the momentum or crash. This reframing gives me agency. I apply influence to the fate of gravity.

I either crash and accept my failure, or I fall and utilize whatever momentum I have in my situation to create something new and keep moving. I've even created moves for positions I often crash from, so I can gracefully bounce out of these positions.

When I crash, people often don't see it. I keep it moving. I plan my falls, creating "bounce back" moves so it looks like I'm not falling. I practice falling. This parallels my creation process in life. Crash and create. Building the plane while flying it. I trust myself when I dance, I embrace failure and use it to do better. Freestyle, throw myself in a direction, trust in my abilities, and see what happens. I ride the momentum and turn it into an opportunity for new discoveries.

Flipping Leadership: Discovery and Reflection

We are not born with the skills it takes to run an organization. They are discovered through the experiences that test us. The "Flipping" sections in this book highlight moments when my leadership and operational skills were tested and what I discovered as a result.

We were learning by doing. I remember when I told my Grampa that I was going to business school, he laughed and asked, "What can a school teach you about business? There are only three things you need to know to be successful in business: buy low, sell high, and watch your overhead." He taught me that learning by doing is the only way. To trust my gut. He often reminded me that he got his education on the corner of University and College, two intersecting streets in

Toronto. In other words, his education came from the streets, not from a classroom.

As we built Unity, we were planting seeds thoughtfully and giving them time, nurturing them, and seeing which ones grew. We ensured that we were open, flexible, and adaptable to the needs of the youth, artists, schools, and communities we were working with. There was no one way that worked; the way was fluid and adaptable, based on the needs of the young people we were there to serve.

The key to our success was prioritization, perseverance, and self-reflection. This did not mean we were just plowing forward with our ideas. We created our programs with members of the communities we served. We listened and learned from the community. We asked for real and honest feedback and altered course based on what we heard from youth, communities, school officials, and artists. We welcomed and encouraged critics in order to keep our ideas growing with integrity. If something was broken in our plane, we needed to acknowledge it and fix it quickly, because, frankly, we were in mid-flight! We were working in a rapidly changing environment, and our success hinged on our integrity. People could smell if we were faking the funk.

In a nutshell, we followed what felt right based on the feedback we were receiving. We had a direction, but not always a set plan. This allowed us to keep meeting the needs of the community as we learned more. We listened to youth to shape the programs, while using hip hop to empower and engage youth to be role models in their communities.

We eventually applied this way of thinking to *every-thing* at Unity — programming, fundraising, financial management, networking, building a board of directors, evaluation, and much more. We tried, we listened, we learned, we evolved, we started again. We just applied the same disciplined principle over and over and never gave up. We were building on the fly. We never took foolish risks, but never stayed static for too long.

I believe that anything that feels too comfortable is dangerous. Being convinced something is and will always be a certain way can prove fatal. When we were comfortable, we often weren't listening and responding to feedback. My natural inclination is to do what is comfortable, things that worked before. I had to constantly push myself out of my comfort zone and stay curious; to test new things or challenge theories I believed to be true. This led to my growth as a leader. What worked in one community did not always work in another. We needed to approach every program like it was our first and review old programs like they had just begun.

Fail Slow, Test Theories, Challenge Assumptions

Unity's first program, outside of those in my own high school, was at Harold M. Brathwaite Secondary School in Brampton. Unity started with a performance in high schools and expanded from one to four schools, then from four schools to twelve schools, in the first four years. We grew through word of mouth and trial and error. I ran across the city to pitch the program to new high schools while still in high school myself. I literally cold-called schools and tried to get the principal on the phone. I would often have to make friends with administrative staff before they would even consider transferring my calls, since most did not want to let anybody speak to the principal. When I could, I tried to find the principal's direct extension and just kept calling it until they answered. I would experiment with different times of the day and eventually determined that principals were more likely to answer the phone at 8:00 a.m., soon after students were in their classes; fifteen minutes after lunch had ended; and fifteen minutes before the end of the school day. I would do anything I could do to get that first meeting: I would even try emailing principals by using their first initial and last name once I knew what school board email addresses worked. Once I had their attention, I would pitch with all my heart to bring our programs into their schools. Eventually, once we had a bit of a track record and testimonials, we had teachers referring us between schools. But in the beginning, I was just a teenager cold-calling with nothing but passion. We were a group of young hip hop artists building programs for and with youth across the city. After a few years, schools asked for more hands-on workshops after the assemblies. Two artists on our team, Matthew "Testament" Jones and Russell "RaSoul" King, test ran emcee workshops, and the students loved them.

We later heard schools wanted their students to perform in the assemblies with our artists to address community-specific issues. These included everything from violence to loss in their community, expressed through hip hop, and we encouraged the fusion of cultural artistic performances and hip hop together.

In response to their request, we created an audition process to include students from each school in our shows. Soon we had bhangra collaborating with hip hop dancers and beatboxers collaborating with violin players, and many more incredible integrations of local culture, art, and youth-driven messages. Then we realized these young people wanted to develop their talents even further, so we created a final showcase at the end of the year for high school student performers from different schools to perform together at one venue. At this event, which we called The Kickoff, youth competed for a scholarship to support their artistic dreams. What began as a small theatre show with an audience of three hundred friends and parents grew into a four-day festival at Toronto's busiest outdoor concert venue at Yonge-Dundas Square with over thirty thousand attendees. Eventually we got major headliners to perform alongside the youth, including Talib Kweli, GZA, Biz Markie, and many others.

As the years went by, we realized we could extend our programs by training Canada's top hip hop artists to teach as Unity Artist Educators. Testament codeveloped Unity's Artist Educator training retreats, which he went on to facilitate for nearly a decade. We launched a weekly after-school program that helped youth express their stress and expand their leadership skills. The idea for the after-school programs came from a spoken-word artist on our roster named Kayin Jeffers. As the youth participants grew up, they told us they were more comfortable in out-of-school programs, so we began to offer community-based programs in partnership with spaces across the city.

I knew our vision had substance: using hip hop to engage and empower youth. We saw the impact. We saw young people in our programs become engaged in music careers after their siblings had been incarcerated. We saw young people stop selling drugs and start earning income through their art. We saw young people engage in their education because they had a new, positive relationship with their high schools and teachers. We saw young people who were horribly bullied become respected amongst their peers and build new friend groups through Unity's programs. We saw young people come out of their shell and become confident in their own skin. The teachers we worked with saw it, the principals in the schools saw it, and our artists saw it. Youth even came back, full circle, as mentors, volunteers, artist educators, and staff. We had tapped into something that many youth programs struggled with: genuine engagement.

I knew hip hop had the power to build community. It helped me as a young person deal with my anxiety and bottled emotions, it helped my breakin' crew who were dealing with their own struggles and personal challenges. Our foundation was strong, yet our path was precarious. A mentor of mine once told me to "fail fast," but that never made sense to me. It felt wrong. I found that when we fully invested ourselves into something over a long period of time that we gave our big ideas the opportunity to succeed or fail with a level of dignity.

For me, I felt failing with dignity was about a much slower, more thoughtful, and invested approach. I believe this is how Unity succeeded. When we rushed the process, we often learned something, but at the expense of time and wasted resources; resources that could have been applied differently and more effectively. Moving quickly, without adequate resources, led to three major initiatives being shelved: all of them good ideas in their own right, but in each case, we didn't follow Unity's slower, more thoughtful, and deeply invested approach, and the opportunities never reached their potential.

The National After-School Program consisted of weekly hip hop–based leadership programs in multiple underserved communities outside of our home city. This program required a ton of operational resources and local experience. We needed someone on the ground in each city to manage these programs, but we did not have the money to scale it effectively. As a result, we were unable to employ enough human resources to execute the same quality we had in our home city, Toronto. We flew into each out-of-town program location once or twice each year to do what we called outreach visits, where our Toronto team would work to build local partnerships, pitch schools, fundraise, and train local artists. We were trying to scale in a cost-effective manner. We never invested in a full-time on-the-ground local manager, and as a result the programs lacked consistency. With a lack of local presence, it became difficult to raise funds in each city. After a few years of trial and error, we scaled back the concept.

We even created something we called National Unity Day to create a celebration at the end of each school year for our programs across Canada. As part of National Unity Day, we hired local artists to run a hip hop cypher event in every major city in Canada on the same day as our festival in Toronto. Again, we didn't provide enough resources to run this to full scale, and it soon fizzled. We landed the plane and put the idea in storage.

The Unity Crew Manual was an ambitious idea, where we wrote and distributed a guide to creating self-sustaining Unity student clubs in high schools. We trusted in youth leaders in high schools to run their own hip hop clubs with a teacher supervisor. We were unable to meet the quality and consistency standards we had set for our programs though, because we didn't have the necessary resources to execute effectively. After two years of trying to implement the Unity Crew Manual in several schools, we decided to put it on the shelf.

While I believe these were all great ideas, we under-resourced them, so they failed. They were side projects that got minimal attention in the organization, and as a result they did not get the support they needed to succeed.

Some of the best opportunities took us several years to nurture, build, and find the right people to lead. It took six years before I really knew if Unity was even worth continuing. If I had given Unity only two years to succeed, it would have died having never seen its full potential. Were there times I felt like giving up? You bet, but I kept pushing because I believed in the core vision of what we were doing.

Journal Entry — March 15, 2010
Winding down from city life and stepping back into my
real self:

Why is it that I only pick up this journal when I travel? It's a mystery to me, but after solidifying our youth breakin' crew called Uniteam, I'd say it is one of my most exciting day-to-day accomplishments within the past 3 months. From coming in 2nd place in their first battle, to representing the entire Steeles L'Amoreaux community in a performance for the mayor, to a Chinese New Year performance that was broadcast to millions of people in China on WowTV, to a 3 part conference for Toronto Public Health and the Lung Association, to winning the organizational pitch competition at the Social Entrepreneurship Exchange conference, to performances in subway stations and on the actual subway as part of TTC's "City on the Move," to teaching 2 classes each week in Malvern and downtown, to running a march break camp, to performing at Second Base Youth Shelter, to performing at Delisle Youth Gallery, to Open Mind spoken word slam at the Hershey Centre, to Loretto Abbey Bandfest, and *the list goes on*!!!

These events, performances, and workshops all happened between January and April of 2010; I can only imagine how this Uniteam group is developing these youth as future leaders. Exciting stuff.

You know what else is exciting? I'm on a tiny plane right now heading to Clyde River, Nunavut. I'm feeling different then my usual nervous. Maybe it'll hit me when I'm over the frozen tundra, but I feel readier for the week ahead of me. I am going to give this week everything I've got working with BluePrintForLife as a dance facilitator. In reality, it's just one more week, a blip in time, but the experiences I have up north and the footprint it leaves behind stick with me. This is by far the most north I will have gone so far in my life. Entering new territory with a new mind-state, open to new experience, which never ceases to pop up amongst the inspiring BluePrint team and incredibly resilient Inuit.

Flipping Leadership: Empower People to Build Things and End Things

In 2010, I decided to start a youth leadership program, as a part of Unity, because I thought the idea had the potential to provide authentic, youth-led programs that would give young people agency to address the things that were directly impacting their lives. Too often adults tell youth what we think they need; with this program, we were giving youth space to drive change themselves. I gathered the top b-boys and b-girls from the high schools in which Unity worked. We met at a coffee shop to discuss if they wanted to create a super group. It was a unanimous *yes*. So we started meeting weekly.

I was driving one of the youths, Tafiya Itiaba Bayah, home after a meeting, and we were having a conversation about the youth leadership group. Tafiya is a young man who is wise beyond his years and from whom I have learned a ton about how I approach the world. He has a deep level of empathy and commitment to supporting his peers and building community. He said to me, "This group, it's like a team, a team that is part of Unity, a . . . Uniteam." We both laughed, and I wrote it on a sticky note and stuck it to my steering wheel. I used sticky notes to track all of the ideas I wanted to follow up on. I had sticky notes everywhere. My rule was if the sticky note fell before I acted on the idea on the note, then it was never meant to be. This note made it to the next meeting, and Uniteam was born!

Uniteam was a group of high-potential youth — b-boys and b-girls, going through their own struggles and successes, but at the same time with a will to give back to their community. I knew this idea had merit — I just didn't know where it would lead. At our second meeting at the coffee shop, I told them, "We can't keep meeting here; we need somewhere to practise. Can anyone find a space for us?" Several members proposed ideas, and at our next meeting we had three options brought to the table by members.

One group member had even written a pitch letter directed at local community centres asking them to donate space for this program. The group made a list of who was going to visit each community centre, and then they were off. After a few weeks, one person came back with a confirmed space. Success! We continued to meet weekly at the new space, a local community centre. At every meeting, I would ask the group, "What do you want to do?" I gave the group members full decision-making power and supported them in any way I could.

After a few weeks, a few members left because the group wasn't for them, and so the remaining members decided to do their own recruiting. They wanted more like-minded leaders who were also great dancers, but the new joiners had to commit. So the youth leaders created a testing ground for new leaders to join the group: Uniteam members would invite candidates to practice sessions, shows, and workshops. They would observe how the new recruits interacted with young people and see if they were open to learning as part of the group. Sometimes candidates would lead warmups in workshops to test their teaching skills. Ultimately, it was about values alignment, and the members of Uniteam treated it like the process of joining a breakin' crew. You don't just get into a crew; you have to get *put down* by the members in the crew based on a matching set of values. In this case, they were testing for young dancers who were serious about breakin', interested in contributing to their community, could use this crew as part of their own personal development, and open to learning. Eventually six candidates were tested, and three were accepted into the fold. All of this happened organically with the simple idea of bringing together young breakers from across the city and allowing them to lead their own program.

The Uniteam members had to secure funding for the group, and so they decided to apply for a grant from Toronto Public Health. It was a five thousand dollar anti-smoking grant to run a youth-led project promoting healthy, smoke-free living. They wrote the application, got accepted into the pitch round, and pitched their idea of teaching dance as a healthy alternative to smoking. The nurses at Toronto Public Health had their minds blown. A few months later, I got a letter from Toronto Public Health with good news: the youth got five thousand dollars to fund their activities!

After securing the grant, Uniteam arranged to use a local dance studio's space for a weekly class where the Uniteam could teach breakin' and raise money to support future activities. But no students showed up for the class, and so, after a few weeks, the studio dropped the program. The dance studio owner was not happy with us as they had higher expectations, but the youth learned a valuable lesson — never over-promise.

Eventually the first core group of leaders from Uniteam moved on to big things in life, often crediting Unity for many of the skills they developed. Skills they were able to develop because they were truly and authentically empowered and trusted.

The second leadership cohort struggled with their commitment to Uniteam, not coincidentally while I began to get busier in building Unity. I was no longer able to meet weekly with the group, so I hired an artist to meet with them in my stead. It just didn't work. The group had an intervention meeting with me and told me they planned to discontinue the group and not recruit another cohort of young leaders.

At first, I really pushed back and suggested hiring another artist to work with them. They pushed back even harder, and they had legitimate arguments to make their case. In their view, the program was no longer having the impact for which it was originally intended. It took them six hours to convince me to come to their way of thinking, and through the process, I learned something powerful from the Uniteam leaders: some things are not meant to live forever. It was time to move forward, and they were fully empowered to not only steer the group but decide when to end it. The impact of Uniteam will last a lifetime, and many of its members went on to entrepreneurial careers, world travels, and great success.

THE UNITY STORY, PART 2: TIMING IS EVERYTHING

Over the years, as Unity evolved, I observed that one of the main reasons we survived through our start-up years was that we provided attention at the right times, in the right ways, to three distinct areas: programs, fundraising, and finance. The programs were first and foremost, as they are the reason we exist. This was the fun part, but, at times, we were guilty of getting lost in the excitement and forgetting about other important areas of the organization.

We started Unity with three people: me doing a little bit of everything; Julla Shanghavi, handling programs and operations; and Malik Musleh, writing grants. Malik was focused on completing at least four grant applications each month. In our early years, it was a bit of a numbers game, but what was most important was we were as invested in fund development as we were in creating and running the best possible programs.

Unfortunately, one critical aspect of operating a non-profit that we overlooked in the early days of Unity was financial management. I was always strong with budgets, and I liked working with numbers, so I did my best. And, at the time when we were a smaller organization, my best was actually good enough.

But in 2008, we were hit with our first audit, and I learned a ton about things I really hadn't understood. It was a huge eye-opener. As we grew as an organization, I began to realize that the complexity of our finances were evolving faster than I could understand them. This got very scary very fast. After a few years of growth, I began to realize I needed to pay equal attention to the finances as I had been paying to fundraising and programming over the years. When we hired for our first full-time position in finance, it was 2013, and because I wanted to save money, I failed to put in place the right support structure and expectations for the role.

In 2014, within one year of hiring our first full-time employee dedicated to finance, Unity had four staff turnovers in its finance administration role, three turnovers in bookkeeping, and two turnovers in board treasurer. It was a living nightmare. Why was this happening? At first, I thought we were choosing the wrong people, but I soon realized two things: I had incorrectly structured the role, and I was underpaying for the position. All of these staff changes led to the books being documented in four different ways in one year. One finance coordinator even lost several months' worth of vital paperwork. It was my biggest nightmare come to life. This led to a very direct and intense management letter from our auditor at the end of the year; a letter that we had to respond to. After reading this seven-page report, I lost over a week of sleep. I felt like a criminal, even though I hadn't done anything wrong.

The turnover of staff left real gaps in our accounting for that year. The auditor had identified areas of risk in Unity's processes for approvals, reimbursements, financial leadership, internal controls, governance, and the list went on. And everything in the report pointed directly back to me and my leadership.

The finance committee, led by our outstanding treasurer, Ugo DiFederico; our board of directors; and our new and amazing finance coordinator, Ella Avila, helped respond to all of these issues with our staff and all associated bookkeeping contractors. Ella was a ray of light in this extremely dark time for me. We updated processes, controls, reporting structures, and staffing. We learned a vital lesson, which was to structure financial management roles with the right expertise and pay people fairly.

At the same time, we were subject to a random audit by one of our largest government funders. To put things in perspective, over the years this one funder had given Unity over a million dollars. At the time of the audit, Unity had two different programs funded by this same funder. They were both called The Hub, but were located in different communities; one in Scarborough and one in Mississauga. Each had its own grant which also meant separate reporting. When we submitted the midterm grant report for the Mississauga Hub, we exported "Hub Program" from QuickBooks and the team submitted it without me knowing.

I later got a notice that this government funder wanted to do a random audit of our grant. Just to double-check, I looked at the numbers in QuickBooks, and I quickly realized we mixed the two locations of Hub programs and multiple grant expenses in one report. We had not actually fully spent the grant and misrepresented this fact in the report we submitted. We had to call the funder and tell them we screwed up. We technically had lied to our biggest funder — and in writing. I lost many nights of sleep leading up to this call. We had underspent the grant and this whole situation led us to redo our entire finance system, including processes, policies, and financial controls. If this wasn't already complicated and stressful enough, we had an equal community partner in the grant, so we had to not only troubleshoot a misrepresented report with the funder but also with a partner. This was a huge learning experience about monthly reporting, integrated systems, open communication, and tracking finances more carefully for every grant. Addressing this was not easy to do, but it was vital to our continued survival and reputation. We had fallen on our face and had to really step up our game.

The various departments at Unity were all growing, but each at its own pace. The main thing they had in common, though, was that they were reactive, rather than proactive, usually responding to getting our hand slapped for not having the right processes in place. When the auditor asked who approved my reimbursements from the charity, we had to establish a cheque-signing policy and what he called a "delegation of authority" approved by the board.

We strengthened the finance department. When we had so many grants and funders that we could no longer keep track of them on paper, we decided to organize them into an Excel spreadsheet. These later became what we learned are called a "prospect list" and a "revenue pipeline." Eventually we had tabs for each city in Canada and each program. Several years later, we upgraded to a donor-management software to track funders and donors. We did our best with what we had at each stage of organizational evolution.

I was so overbooked in programs that I did not have enough time to fundraise. I had to stop performing in Unity programs as an artist and hired a program manager. It was hard for me to embrace my evolving role, but our programs grew and grew stronger.

One small step at a time, Unity grew, each respective department grew, and new departments popped up: programs, fundraising, finance, evaluations, event planning, artist training — and the list goes on. But once we grew to over fifteen paid staff, I realized there was a new problem. Each department had developed itself as a strong independent unit that "knew what it was doing," but I soon learned they didn't know what the other departments were doing. We had become completely siloed.

For example, a big funding opportunity came up to launch new after-school programs in Brampton and Mississauga. The funding team submitted a grant without fully consulting the programs team; when the funding was received, this project became one of the most challenging for the programs team, taking time and resources from all of their other work. A glaring lack of communication had real consequences. As a result, we embarked on building bridges between the funding, finance, and programs teams. At first this was like pulling teeth: after having done their jobs a certain way for years, nobody wanted to have to add another step by consulting someone in another department before making a decision.

But change had to happen, because if the funding team promised in a grant proposal that the programs team would run a program, then the program would have to fit the vision and capacity of the programs team in that moment and beyond. Also, we would need the finance team to be able to report on the expenses and help with exporting budgets for each program department accurately. This way the funding team would know how much money still needed to be raised, and the programs team would know when they could start new programs and when they needed to cut back.

These bridges started other conversations that were even more exciting. For example, program sustainability actually has a lot to do with funding sustainability. So, when the funding team began to understand this, they would not push to start new programs but to create funding strategies that would sustain current programs or the highest need, most successful programs. Building bridges also built new levels of understanding and accountability.

This may seem obvious, but the execution is easier said than done. First, getting the budget formatted so that it was a separated profit and loss for each program took almost three years before it was fully operational. Once the separation occurred, we generated quarterly financial reports for each program so we could make decisions based on real numbers.

Building that bridge between programs, finance, and fundraising was vital during Unity's growth. Obviously, it's the people who run all of this, but once great people are in place, they need to start talking to each other in systematic ways that make all their jobs easier and more successful. Ultimately, it's about the whole being successful, not just the individual parts.

Finance and Growth: The Chicken and the Egg

How do you grow an organization without the means to do it? The risk is paying fixed costs in a start-up with no guaranteed revenue. This was my constant chicken-and-egg dilemma at every phase, whenever a small burst of growth happened. If we invested in a new staff member, could we still make payroll? Would we still be able to afford the new hire a year down the road? We were always conservative in our spending and kept our costs to a minimum, all the while gauging our worth by our output.

In my opinion, I see a lot of inefficiency in the non-profit sector, and this has motivated me to produce high-quality programs while keeping a careful eye on the budget. How could we best respond to a community's need and figure out precisely how much money we needed to do so? As non-profit leaders, we need to strongly consider the question, "How much is enough to meet the needs of the communities we serve?" This is not an infinite number. It is like going to a buffet and eating until you are full. Your stomach tells you when to stop. If fundraisers say there is no ceiling to what is needed, then they may need to re-evaluate the clarity of their mission. Unfortunately, the funding pie has not grown in proportion to the issues that are plaguing the world, let alone our local communities.

It was incumbent on us to master fundraising, and also to master budgeting. I love budgets as they tell the real story of what is happening in the now, in the real world. Studying the financial picture taught me to be resourceful, creative, and factual. I learned when and what to cut, if I had to. More importantly, I grew to understand what was required to keep the team employed and programs running at high efficiency and effectiveness. I knew where to cut costs without losing quality.

Our programs had to be high quality to be deemed worthy to grow. By 2011, we were running day-long engagements in schools, after-school programs held weekly in underserved neighbourhoods, and community-based leadership development programs all using hip hop as a tool to engage youth. We would pull apart and analyze every program to see what went right and what could be done better. Any programs struggling with engagement, retention, or good anecdotal feedback, we would revise. Why would we scale a program before we were certain of validated and relatively consistent results?

We had to go beyond counting numbers, so we began to design program evaluation surveys, both qualitative and quantitative. Growing a program before knowing it has impact or potential is dangerous. Programs can cause harm if grown irresponsibly. We quickly learned about evaluation from a few key mentors who were experts in the space, and we began to launch survey tools, focus groups, and projects to help us measure the impact we were having. We created an evaluation committee with youth, staff, and experts in evaluation, including Shane Green, who worked for Grand Challenges Canada, evaluating innovative mental health programs internationally; Sarah Earl, the director of program research and development at YMCA; and several other evaluation experts. Shane, Sarah, and the entire committee were all key players in helping us to co-create a responsive impact measurement system for the organization that was producing useful and actionable data.

Each burst of growth was followed by asking myself if we could sustain this growth and did we have multiple reliable relationships with funders to help sustain it. I didn't want to risk what we didn't have. I also knew better than to put at risk what we did have, which was an impeccable reputation, which had been built because of our amazing artists and team.

Despite the huge engine that powers fundraising in the healthcare sector, for example, we know that there are not enough dollars to meet the needs of those we seek to serve. We need to be effective with the funds we raise and ask difficult questions around how much is enough. We at Unity made stewardship a priority, as we were accountable to the donors and the wider sector. We needed to demonstrate public accountability. To solicit money for programs to serve a need that cannot be defined and an impact that cannot be measured flies in the face of accountability. To serve our community and donors, we needed to be incredibly resourceful, allocate our budgets wisely, pay people fairly, and punch above our weight to get attention. Sometimes it felt like an uphill battle, but we kept our heads up, kept learning, and moved things forward.

Finding the right measurement tool is hard. For example, we, along with Social Venture Partners Toronto (more on this story on page 79), tried to calculate a social return on investment (SROI) for Unity. This is a dollar value assigned to how much money a program like Unity could save for society as a result of the impact we had on youth we served. After many meetings and calculations, we learned that this SROI was not an appropriate metric for our organization. We focused our work upstream on prevention by building resilience in youth living in underserved communities. We defined "underserved" to include neighbourhoods that had significant barriers for youth to achieve their full potential and communities that had a lack of access to engaging arts-based programs. We couldn't calculate a clean number that was entirely attributable to Unity, so we no longer tried to measure by that standard. We learned our work was about contribution, not attribution. We were contributing to a solution, we weren't the solution. We took what we learned from this experiment and applied it to measurement tools we later built ourselves.

Flipping Operations: Scenarios for Sustainability

I remember the biggest chicken-and-egg moment came when the board asked me to create a compensation grid in 2011 after three years of being a registered charity. This would capture the target salaries for all of our staff, at that time and for the next three years. As I began work on the project, I realized we would need a strong fiscal foundation to sustain it. I created three scenarios of a three-year compensation plan: optimistic, pessimistic, and realistic. Looking at them on paper, they all seemed out of reach. I crunched the numbers of potential donors and how I saw us growing. The exercise served as a tool to motivate me to raise more money.

I knew we needed to pay people fairly; it was a core principle of our mission. I remember the time we posted a job opening — when I shared it with an executive director of another charity, they refused to share the posting because it would depress salaries in the sector. In our early years, it was the best we could do. This really struck a nerve with me. I knew we needed to be better and pay salaries above the average in the industry. It seemed like setting an impossible goal, but it lit a fire under my ass to get there, and we surpassed our fundraising targets every year after that for over a decade.

I was always frantically cross checking the budgets, compensation grid, organizational chart, and quarterly reports to ensure we weren't falling short. I qualified every potential donor in our revenue pipeline: 10 percent chance if they told us it was unlikely; 25 percent if they were a first-time ask that was very competitive. We defined a *competitive donor* as one that awards money to less than 10 percent of applicants. Sometimes a funder would tell us outright that the application process was "very competitive," and, over time, we learned that this might be code for "we only support charities with whom we have an existing relationship."

It is this subtext that helped us qualify likely donors. We had to learn to read between the lines: 50 percent if they have given to us before but told us it was competitive; 75 percent if they have given year after year and seemed likely to give again; and 100 percent if they had confirmed multi-year support. I would then multiply the dollar amount we applied for by the percentage I had applied, to get a rough expectation of how much money we would have by the end of that year. This was a constant exercise, but one that was necessary to help me sleep.

When I didn't feel confident that the confirmed revenue would cover our budget, I would recalculate our revenue pipeline. If there was a shortfall, I would drive donations, fundraising, and earned revenue from school and corporate programs until we were in a stable position. Over time, this process became a relatively accurate predictor of how much revenue we could count on, even though more than half of our entire budget was unconfirmed at the beginning of each year.

Each budget increase was a gamble. If I made a jump to increase expenses that would hopefully produce more revenue, would I be able to sustain it? If I couldn't sustain it, what would I do? Cut somewhere else? Raise more money? This is why we grew conservatively but very thoughtfully. Always having cost efficiency in mind while driving fundraising at full force was what kept this equation in balance.

Our strategy was to not rush growth: slow, conservative growth based on realistic projections; a team culture like no other; and quality programming. This is what grew Unity.

Unity grew from 13 percent to 200 percent every year for ten years of audited financial statements from 2008 to 2017:

Year	Annual Expenses
2008	$41,000
2009	$123,000
2010	$139, 000
2011	$275,000
2012	$513,000
2013	$676,000
2014	$915,000
2015	$1,046,000
2016	$1,193,000
2017	$1,411,000

Overall, a 3,341 percent increase over ten years. Each year ended with a revenue surplus that Unity eventually developed into a "rainy day" fund with a board policy on its intended use.

Pressure Points of Growth

Another key to Unity's success was making critical changes as the organization evolved. For example, when we first started Unity, we could only sell our programs to individual schools through teacher champions; but as we grew, we were able to establish fully funded partnerships with school boards based on our established track record. Our program staff had to learn to sell a holistic experience instead of trying to make a sale of a one-off Unity Day event. By researching, listening, and understanding the needs of the community, they were able pitch a custom-fit offering in the form of year-long after-school programs structured to address specific community needs.

At the same time, our board of directors transitioned from one composed of a group of capable individuals ranging from friends to high-level executives, to a defined, competency-based board that added strategic value, established governance, and contributed to Unity's growth. While our board evolved, so too did our organizational chart, moving from staff managing multiple roles in the beginning to specific and well-defined job functions. At one point, we had one employee in charge of fundraising, communications, HR, evaluation, and community partnerships, as well as managing multiple staff members. This was clearly not a sustainable, or even reasonable, job description.

I look at these moments as "pressure points" — when the pressure is building in one area and we know we must change something before it bursts. Our ability to make those changes came down to resources: do we have the time, money, and capacity to grow to meet a need where it is most urgent? This was always a tough balancing act, but vital in choosing which pressure points to focus on at what time.

In 2007 we made the decision to become an independent organization — breaking away from LOVE — as we knew we needed autonomy to grow our vision beyond just a single program. We needed to have authority over decision-making in order to spread our programs to new communities in a responsive way. Our team had a unique way of working together, and we needed space to build on this and not be limited by the decision-making of a parent organization. We went through six different forms of registration over the five years from 2003 to 2007 (from an unregistered volunteer group, to student club, to program of a charity, to trusteed, to non-profit, to charity), until we realized we needed our own organization to fulfil our mission. We decided we wanted to take the organization to the next level, so we chose to create something more permanent.

To restate a bit of history, we started as an unincorporated group of passionate volunteers and artists in 2003. Later I joined the board of directors of a charity called Leave Out ViolencE (LOVE). Our work became a program at LOVE in 2004. LOVE let me join their board, and for three years I learned the inner workings of a non-profit and charity. Their executive director, Lana Feinstein, was a huge mentor to me at the time.

When I went to university in 2005, we registered as a Student Club called LOVE at York University, which we later renamed to Unity at York. Unity became a registered student club at York, and all of our funding came from campus. We recruited a pool of dedicated student volunteers and got an office space for free in the student centre. As I was approaching graduation, I decided to register Unity as a national non-profit with the intention of becoming a registered charity and sustaining our work in the long term. At this point, we felt our work was unique enough to be an independent organization. We evolved again. In 2007, a few donors were interested in donating to Unity but requested a tax receipt for their support, so we made an agreement to be trusteed by a charity called Phoenix Community Works Foundation (PCWF). In between graduating from university and becoming our own registered charity, PCWF held Unity's funds: around $40,000 in total from donations and grants.

When we applied for charitable status, we waited nine months for Canada Revenue Agency (CRA) to even look at our application. CRA has a rule that it needs to look at all applications within nine months from date of submission. On the first day of the ninth month, I called CRA to check on the status of our application, and they told me an update had been mailed. We got denied and had to revise our application. We hired a different lawyer to help us with the process the second time: the lawyer we used for the first application used an articling student to handle all our paperwork. Lesson learned! We waited another stressful five months until Unity's charitable status arrived. Once again, Unity had evolved under the pressure points of growth and was ready to move into the next phase of its evolution, now as a registered charitable organization.

Back to the Basement

Right from the beginning, Unity's guiding principle was to engage communities, youth, and artists to design and create our programs based on the needs of the youth we served. Self-awareness and listening to our various communities created new levels of opportunity for growth for Unity and for me personally. As Unity grew, I gradually learned how to let go of my ego and began to welcome more honest, unfiltered feedback from our team.

We would meet monthly in my basement with anyone from the team who wanted to contribute to what was going on. We had artists, volunteers, board members, community members, teachers, and more. We called it "back to the basement" mainly because we met in a basement, but also because it sounded cool. It was our way of truly listening to the community, our clients, and responding to their needs in real time. It was a powerful and responsive feedback loop in an informal, unfiltered environment.

Flipping Operations: You Don't Work for Unity — You Are Unity

One thing that evolved in the basement was Unity's comprehensive code of conduct for working with youth. We believed first and foremost in safety for all. The code of conduct defined how we would work with youth. After a few years of applying the code of conduct, we realized that as we trained our artist educators and frontline staff, it was framed in a negative way. It told us everything we couldn't do, but we were hearing from our team that they wanted to understand what they could do and what Unity expected them to do — the dos and not just the don'ts. This was challenging because we needed to be clear on areas that were often grey and blurry in many ways. For example, if we worked with a youth in Unity and ten years later we see them in a bar once they are of legal age, what do we do? Do we leave the bar? Do we pretend like we don't see them? Do we say hi? Do we drink while in their presence? Do we buy them a drink? We would discuss these blurred lines at length, some more obvious, some less so. What is our protocol on hugging? These were sensitive yet critical conversations to have amongst the team so no assumptions were made and expectations were clear. In doing so, we created a safer environment for the youth we served and for our staff and artists.

Over several months we gathered the opinions of artists, frontline staff, and social workers on the so-called grey zone moments. We took the former code of conduct and updated it with new language and real scenarios. We learned that it was all incredibly contextual. As a result, we developed a brand-new Unity code of conduct for working with youth. We created this with the support of two professionals in the field of social work, Ellen Sue Mesbur and Lynne Mitchell. The final document became a key part of Unity's training program for all staff. The code's guidelines are framed in Unity's values, ethics, and protocol. It's a living document, Unity's compass, not just a boilerplate policy. We embodied the code of conduct in our actions, and it evolved as our organization grew. We included the code as a qualification in our frontline job postings and interviewed with an eye to an alignment with Unity values and ethical judgment when working with youth.

The basement was a testing ground for creating and challenging new ideas. This was the space to dream big and bring new ideas to life. I often said to the team, "You don't work for Unity; you are Unity." Our people were our driving force, and by listening to their ideas the team stayed involved and engaged. These meetings contributed a great deal to Unity's growth, from our mission statement to creating the curriculum for our after-school program.

Later in Unity's program evolution, we began focusing our impact on using hip hop to improve youth mental health and well-being. This focus felt like a natural progression. Remember, our tagline was "express your stress." We were using hip hop as a tool to build resilience in youth. We wanted to target mental health as one of the root causes of many social ills facing youth today. This required new training, new partnerships, additional support, and more resources for artists, staff, and youth. Again, we began to reinvent ourselves while staying true to the needs of our community. We were growing our grassroots and continued to lead with our values of respect, passion, integrity, community, and youth.

We also began working outside of schools to achieve deeper relationships and outcomes with the youth we were serving. We formed a partnership with the City of Toronto Youth Outreach Workers to run leadership programs in underserved Toronto communities. This program was the perfect match with Unity, as the outreach workers were bringing youth into the community centres and looking for creative leadership programs to better engage them.

This collaboration met our joint objectives of connecting with and serving youth living in underserved neighbourhoods and engaging in large-scale city-wide collaborations. Together we created greater impact for the community. We both did what we did best and were able to provide a valuable service to the community, proving that partnerships can produce powerful outcomes if matched and managed correctly.

These programs were co-developed by Clinton Ghosh, Unity's after-school program manager, and Adrian Chan, Unity's after-school program coordinator. Clinton and Adrian soon realized even these ten-week City of Toronto partnered programs weren't enough. After the ten weeks ended, the youth were still showing up to the community centre but no longer had the facilitated programming. So we began offering community programs year-round. We then realized some youth were coming back to these community-based programs year after year, so our team began offering alumni roles as mentors, enabling them to continue to contribute in a meaningful way. When it occurred to us these mentors needed jobs, we began hiring youth as artist educators and providing paid mentorships.

One evolution led to another until we had a multi-faceted high-impact program, but it didn't happen overnight. We just kept responding to the emerging needs of each group of youths we worked with, one iteration at a time. As their needs changed, we adapted our programming. Flexibility was built into our structure.

Together with our community, artists, youth, staff, and alumni, we developed Unity's mission, values, culture, evaluation process, strategic plan, and branding. It was vital that Unity was co-created and always evolving. This was the secret sauce: Unity wasn't an institution — it was a community, a movement.

Cat: My Best Risks Were Taken on People with Integrity

In 2014, I received an email from Catherine "Cat" Turcotte, asking about getting involved with Unity. Cat was a hip hop dancer who had just moved to Toronto from Montreal to go to school. Cat went to York University and was part of the Community Arts for Social Change program. She seemed super eager and excited to connect, so we did.

I remember meeting Cat at a local coffee shop and just being floored by her passion and charisma. I knew she represented the values of Unity from the moment I met her. She expressed to me that when she finished school she wanted to be a part of the Unity team. I thought giving her a volunteer role would be a good place to start her connection to the crew, so I gave her the most important volunteer role I could think of.

The Unity Festival has one volunteer role that is pivotal to the success of the entire event. The person who drives the big truck to the venue with all of the supplies, gear, and really everything needed to run the festival is crucial, and this was no easy job. The driver had to always arrive before everyone else while navigating this huge vehicle in busy downtown Toronto traffic and narrow streets.

For some reason, on first meeting, I decided to ask Cat if she wanted to take on this vital volunteer job, even though it had very little to do with her interest in working with community. I don't know why, but I knew she could do it. Her genuine passion for youth work beamed from her throughout our meeting. I remember telling her, "I don't know why, but I trust you."

Cat agreed to drive the truck, even though what she really wanted to do was her student placement at Unity for her Community Arts course to work with youth and develop programs. What I didn't know was Cat took this task more seriously than I could have ever imagined. She went home to Montreal to practise driving trucks with her father, who was a transport driver. Cat later told me she rented an even larger truck than the one she would be driving for Unity for this purpose. Her dad even got her to drive this massive rental truck backwards in zigzags between pylons. She didn't hit one!

The next year, she did her Community Arts program internship with Unity. Cat re-engaged Unity alumni and volunteers and developed Unity's community programs model. At first, we brought Cat on to the artist educator roster on contract at Unity.

We eventually created a job for community programs coordinator with Cat in mind. Cat built Unity's community programs from the ground up. As a strong advocate for community development, she brought in the voice of youth, artists, and underrepresented communities every step of the way. Cat transformed Unity's approach to programming. She developed programs based on need, asking youth what they wanted and surveying artists on how to authentically represent hip hop culture in programs. Cat even designed and implemented evaluations done entirely through movement and dance in partnership with our evaluations committee.

She brought her experience as a hip hop dancer and community developer — along with a deeply empathetic personality — to her role as community programs coordinator. Many youth in Cat's community programs grew up with Unity and came full circle with us, becoming mentors, alumni, and artist educators. She was fostering a generation of creative, resilient young leaders through mentorship and empowerment. She even helped develop and implement key parts of Unity's artist and staff training on anti-oppression practices, intersectionality, and community development.

I believed in Cat and in turn she surpassed every expectation I could have dreamed of. I knew she could do it, I just didn't know what "it" was. I trusted Cat with the direction of Unity's vision because I knew she had a gift in programming. She taught me what true community development looks like and continued to remind me of the importance of involving participants, artists, and community directly into Unity's strategy, training, curriculum, and evaluation, and on its board.

SHIFTING FROM A SCARCITY MINDSET TO AN ABUNDANCE MINDSET

Too many charities have a scarcity mindset. Starting from a place of deficit, non-profits often run purely on funding from donors or even worse, a single major government funder. This model allows for mediocrity, which is a proposition I do not accept. The sector deserves better, our staff deserve better, our community deserves better. It is our responsibility to diversify revenue so we can best serve our mission.

Through providing resources staff needed for programs to succeed and have impact, Unity created a mentality of abundance. I wanted the team to truly believe that anything was possible.

This was a sensitive dance. This did not mean a lack of fiscal responsibility or spending money we didn't have. In fact, this attitude made the team more fiscally aware. We had a "spend conservatively" motto at Unity, saving dollars wherever it was possible while maintaining the integrity of the programs and paying people fairly.

To me this abundance mentality set the tone for our culture: being innovative without holding back. If there was a good case that could be made to strengthen the programs, we found a way to make it happen.

I led by example, so the team learned that if I was hustling to keep this ship afloat, they had better be doing the same. There was a powerful and unspoken sense of responsibility amongst the team, amplified by the impact they saw through their individual contributions. Our team took great pride in their work. Abundance empowered us to do what we felt were the right things for the youth we served, and do it in a timely manner. This was pivotal: we did have an approval process for financing out-of-budget ideas, but it didn't take more than a few days, sometimes no more than a few hours, for me to give the go-ahead on new initiatives or pilot projects. We needed to be responsive in addition to being resourceful. If we live in scarcity, we perpetuate limits on the communities we serve.

If we thought testing a small idea would tell us something important that could yield improvements, like providing transportation for youth to get to the programs, or bringing in food, we would try it. When we brought in food, program attendance and engagement went up. Youth were hungry after school. So, we took this small test and implemented it across all programs. We partnered with Second Harvest, an organization that provided donated food to people, organizations, and communities in need, and they provided snacks, year-round, to all of our after-school programs. We saw a need, tested an idea, and scaled the idea resourcefully once we saw success. This is how we built our plane while flying it.

I tried to never make the team feel like they didn't have the resources to do their job well. At the same time, I had to continually recalculate the budget and revenue pipeline to ensure that was actually possible. I had to always be far ahead of the budget and cash flow. This was the pulse of the organization.

Flipping Sustainability: The Innovation Fund

The belief in abundance at Unity allowed us to make the decisions we needed to in order to do the right thing for the youth we served. In the history of Unity, we never stopped a program due to lack of funds. It was our duty to not cancel programs if youth were meaningfully engaged in them. We once ran a program for youth living on the margins in partnership with an organization called SKETCH Working Arts. We did so for almost two years without any funding. This program sometimes had only five youths in attendance, but the program provided an important outlet for them, so we kept running it even though it was in the red. Eventually we did find a donor, but before we did, we tightened up budgets and put pressure on the fundraising team to move the program forward. Over the years, there were other programs where we ran at a loss, but because we had saved money in other budgets and had enough unallocated funding, we were able to keep them afloat. We were constantly taking the pulse of each individual part of Unity in order to maintain the abundance mindset.

Eventually I renamed this unallocated funding pool the "innovation fund." I went after donors to provide flexible funding to test new ideas and quickly respond to needs as we saw them. We told them to trust us with their funds as we were the experts in listening to, testing with, and learning from the communities we worked for. The innovation budget gave us a buffer to try things out even when we didn't have the budgets to do so. It gave our team space to play and test their theories in real time when they identified something that could be improved. It gave us space to dream.

I believe abundance needs to also be reflected in staff compensation in the non-profit and charitable sectors. We often lose top talent because we are unable to pay people what they deserve. Some go to higher paying corporate jobs, but unfortunately many just burn out. I'm proud of where Unity landed in terms of compensation, but not proud of where we started. We went through an evolution in the first five years when we were trying to keep afloat as an organization and still pay our staff. After over a decade of low salaries, we raised our compensation levels above industry standards based on benchmark reports. In the first few years, I was getting paid the same as every other staff member; I felt that if we were going to do this work for minimum wage, then we should all be in it together.

This sense of equality kept the team committed to the larger vision even if the pay was unreasonably low at first. I wanted to pay people more, but simply did not have the money to do so. As it was, we were barely making payroll each month. It was either we paid people what we could or close down. Some people wouldn't even share our job postings because the pay was so low. It was always my goal that one day we would be able to pay people a living wage, and I knew we would get there. Each year, depending on how well we did, I increased everyone's salary by one to ten thousand dollars, and I continued doing so until we surpassed the industry standard for salaries.

It was my commitment that staff compensation would always grow with the organization based on what we could afford. Just before we hit one million dollars in revenue, I decided to add health and dental benefits, bonuses, and several other incentives. We also paid for part of staff transportation, and eventually even got them company phones and plans. We paid for a work laptop for each staff member as well. Although all of this stuff probably sounds obvious, we had to hustle to find the funding to keep the programs running and to properly support the people who ran this organization.

When Unity first started we didn't have a ton of money, but we chose carefully where to invest it. One thing I was always proud of was that we paid our artist educators above industry standard and we paid the artists as soon as they stepped off the stage or completed a workshop. This was my personal commitment to respecting the people who were doing the frontline work. Many emerging and established hip hop artists told me that the money from Unity gigs was the base income that allowed them to quit their jobs and commit to their art full time. We created abundance amongst our frontline artists through genuine respect for their craft and commitment.

There is a real chicken-and-egg process to growth: it seems impossible to prioritize where to invest first when you have limited or no funds. Money doesn't fall from the sky, and every time we invested in something, we had to develop a new and consistent revenue stream to sustain it. Bottom line: our team was more likely to get what we needed if we were willing to do the work to get it, believed it was worth it, and understood why it was important.

SHARE YOUR SECRET SAUCE

Whether we like to admit it or not, the non-profit sector is competitive. There is a spoken and unspoken protectiveness around intellectual property as it relates to programming, resources, and research in charities. I think this is bullshit. Charities should operate to help solve problems that exist in the world, not out of self-interest. By sharing our secret sauce with each other, we can have far greater impact for the people we serve than we can working in isolation and guarding resources. Making a sustained and responsible impact is not about being the best or the biggest. It is about working towards a collective mission. Collaboration is needed now more than ever to combat the world's most pressing challenges.

Our work is a small part of a bigger social picture. The work is interconnected and interrelated. Working together, we can create responsible and respectful change. Working alone, we create new problems. We need to put our impact before our egos. We need to stop hoarding great ideas with the goal of keeping our organizations alive. We need to think about the bigger picture.

We need to know what we do well, do what we do well, and find collaborative partners to fill the gaps of what we don't do well. I have had direct meetings with funders and donors who encourage and finance collaboration. The missing link is we need to teach the sector how to work together better. The problem is the system falsely incentivizes competitive mindsets of scarcity over collaborative mindsets of abundance. We are caught chasing funds instead of truly trying to make change. In addition, I believe the real solutions are found in more cross-sector collaboration between non-profits, governments, corporations, communities, and individuals.

At Unity, we tried to embody a collaborative versus a competitive mentality. Partnerships worked well when we embraced the purpose of creating greater impact together.

Imagine a world where we could share resources, people, and ideas across multiple charitable organizations. Imagine the impact this could have both from a beneficiary and financial perspective. Anything at Unity that I believed could add value to the sector, I would share openly with other organizations and artists, here in Canada and around the world. An authentic and well-matched partnership can be a transformative experience for the team, and more importantly create something completely unexpected that can have an exponentially larger impact. On the flip side, a partnership with falsely aligned values or mismatched corporate culture can be a disaster.

I shared Unity's model with organizations in Sweden, the Netherlands, Italy, and Japan. I saw hybrids of our programs sprout up all over the world, run by local hip hop artists and organizers. Not everything needs to be branded and claimed.

I was once contacted by an organization in a small community in northern Sweden running a dance camp. They invited me to their city,

Älvsbyn, to share Unity's model. I shared everything I could in program curriculum, artist training, organizational structure, fundraising, and more. Several months later they launched a funded hip hop school program in three schools in Sweden. All I did was share our model and approach openly. I believe we need to share knowledge more freely, because knowledge is power.

A Partnership between Unity and
Boost Child & Youth Advocacy Centre

In 2015, Unity entered into a partnership with Boost Child & Youth Advocacy Centre through meetings with its executive director Karyn Kennedy. Karyn saw something in what we did and invited me to present at a staff meeting. I shared the Unity story with Boost staff, who expressed strong interest in our work. A few months later, Karyn invited me to another meeting; actually, she insisted that I attend it. The meeting was a discussion around a major federal government grant that Boost was thinking of applying for to create a trauma-informed dance therapy program, a program they hoped to run in a three-way partnership: Unity would design and deliver the dance curriculum, Ryerson University would do the research, and Boost would bring in social workers who were expertly trained in supporting young people who had experienced trauma and would manage the intake process for participants.

The goal of the research was to measure the impact that dance therapy had in conjunction with traditional care for youth who had suffered from trauma. This federal government grant was from Health Canada and was the type of funding for which only very established organizations are invited to apply. Unity would never have received an opportunity to apply for this type of funding if it weren't for the partnership request from Boost. We agreed to enter the partnership, and Boost and Ryerson collaborated on writing the grant application. We reviewed it and approved our involvement, not fully realizing the magnitude of what we were stepping into.

A few months went by, and the grant was not top of mind at Unity as we were incredibly busy with our regular programs and operations. Then, all of a sudden, we got an email from Karyn — we were approved! There was lots of immediate celebration, but then we started to ask ourselves, what does this actually mean for us in the coming years? We started looking into the details, and, wow, it was much bigger than we had anticipated and meant providing services in locations that surprised us. I didn't remember agreeing to programs in Orillia, a two-hour drive from the city. Maybe it was buried in the hundred or so pages of the grant application. Our team had a bit of a panic moment. What had we signed ourselves up for? Taking on a commitment of this size could have a negative impact on our organization if we failed to manage the workload.

We were stepping into the unknown with trepidation, but also with open hearts and open minds. We went to the first few meetings just to listen and ask questions. We knew we were in over our heads, but we were ready to rise to the occasion and learn on the fly once again. We soon discovered this program actually had an intensive research project as its core focus. It took us all six months to co-write a forty-page curriculum and create the surveys, promotion strategy, and intake processes, which then needed research ethics approval from Ryerson University. This development process was led by Cat and Rachael Edge, a.k.a. "Redge," from Unity in collaboration with Boost's staff, who work with youth through a trauma-informed lens. A few weeks passed. We got ethics approval! Everyone celebrated again.

Finally, we launched the program in January 2017. We had a successful first group but realized we needed to focus more on recruitment to engage more youth over the course of the project: we had to reach approximately three hundred youth over five years for the research study, and we were already behind. The key to this partnership was communication and trust. There were tons of meetings to pick up the pieces and answer the tough questions we didn't see coming. But we came to the meetings with the right questions, pushed back where we felt we needed more support, and agreed to disagree at times. We had solidarity in our goals, even though at times we had different ways of operating.

The experience with Boost and Ryerson taught me a ton about what it takes to make a partnership work, and what I learned is that it's a lot of work! You must ask for what you need and clarify what you don't understand especially when it's so vast in scale, scope, and expectation. Boost was amazing to work with, and thankfully this allowed us to get through some difficult conversations around timelines, budget revisions, scaling programs, and much more. The key to success was our alignment in values and a shared desire for meaningful and responsible impact.

Partnership Fundamentals: Respect, Communication, Trust

Sharing your secret sauce doesn't always work out, but that doesn't mean that we shouldn't do it. We really learned through mistakes and failures as this story shows. n 2010, Unity got a call from an organization based in Western Canada. I had met one member of this organization at a recent conference, and we talked about how Unity managed expanding our programs to meet the needs of communities. The organization asked if we would be interested in doing two weeks of our Unity Day program for middle schools and high schools in their region.

As part of our partnership agreement, they sourced the funding and dealt with all program logistics and flew six members of our team out west to run the program. From the beginning there were red flags around their transparency on funding, and we saw high staff turnover, which was also a big concern. Unfortunately, instead of asking questions and pushing back, I failed to scale Unity responsibly. I chose to ignore the red flags and Unity continued with the relationship, coordinating and executing local artist training and running Unity Day school programs in partnership with them for several years.

In 2015, the organization told us our services were no longer needed to run the school program. We were cut out. We found out they had raised a ton of money from government and corporate supporters and planned to continue the program we started together, now without us. Even though we were happy to have inspired a local project outside of our home, it had misaligned values, which ultimately trickled into the work. When we got booted out of our own program, we began to realize it was equally our fault for not speaking up.

Now a program lives on without us under an organization that did not align with our values. We gave birth to something that we could not control. Although we felt burned by the situation, I learned something very important: we need to fully trust and align with the partners with whom we work, and we must communicate when we feel uncomfortable. In a strange and conflicted way, I am still happy to know that the program continues without us, even though it doesn't fully reflect the values and vision of Unity. After this experience, we learned to only align with partners whose values and corporate culture were in lockstep with Unity's.

Eventually Unity went on to create a community partnership framework that qualified potential partners based on need and match. Rajni Sharma took this on as part of her job to create a long list of partners to source and engage. We had three levels of partners, characterized by the amount of time it would take to nurture the partnership: high-, medium-, and low-involved. We had a list of items we would look for in community partnerships including in-kind space, funding, programming expertise, evaluation support, research support, youth referrals, shared resources, and staffing. If a partnership had only one of these items, then it would be low-involved. If it had two of these items, it would be a medium-involved partnership. And, if a partnership had three or more of these items, it would be high-involved.

For example, Boost was a high-involved partner, involving research, curriculum design, implementation in multiple locations, national government funding, shared staff, and much more. As a result, the Boost partnership required more staff time and involvement to ensure we stayed on track. There were monthly partnership meetings as well as multiple weekly programs. On the other hand, the partnership we had with the Art Gallery of Ontario (AGO) was much simpler: AGO provided Unity with space for our free weekly breakin' programs and with some funding to support our artist educators who ran them. This required only semi-annual check-in meetings to ensure things were on track. We matched partnerships based on what we needed as an organization to achieve our mission. We looked for best-matched partners who had what we were looking for, and vice versa.

It was all about mutual benefit and impact potential. This process helped us find the most compatible community partners and leverage resources further without re-creating services that already existed. Eventually Unity was working with over thirty community partners, providing everything from mental health referral services for youth to in-kind space, to evaluation support, to nutritious food in programs.

Journal Entry — July 15, 2010
On a plane to the Yukon with Uniteam:

Wow. I wish I had more time to write in this bad boy but almost 2 months since my last entry and here I am, on a plane to the Yukon with 10 breakers and 3 youth from the Uniteam crew. After just getting back from a 12 hour road trip to Montreal and Quebec City with Uniteam, I'm starting to feel oddly, fatherly . . . It's weird when you are fully responsible for other people's kids. You really learn how responsible a parent you'll be (and how irresponsible). In all honesty, though, I'm starting to really feel and understand the power of being a role model and mentor to young people. They really do remember *everything* you say and do. Sometimes I'll say something and they will remind me for weeks. You are really put in a no bullshit position. I am not here to be a fake goody two shoes and censor my behaviour. In fact, the more I'm really honestly and openly me, the more I feel the members of Uniteam feel comfortable to be who they really are. Not the front they put on for their parents or teachers but just them. I'm learning more and more that if I am always striving to just react the way my mind and body tell me naturally, then I find myself surrounded by the right people for me. Meaning my natural, honest, and true self will attract people of complementary mindsets and attitudes. The people who don't accept you for you can choose not to be associated with you. Slowly, I've developed a group of friends and even a team with Unity that shares a similar free attitude towards life, with a positive mindset and a passion for art to heal. The energy I put out into the world is the energy that comes back, tenfold.

THE VALUE OF MENTORS

In the beginning while we were building Unity, we didn't use a methodical process. We acted on what we felt was right. In fact, because we coined ourselves as a *youth-led* group, it almost felt like we couldn't ask for advice from adults. We very quickly grew out of this mindset, mainly because we were growing up ourselves. We also realized we could grow faster and smarter by learning from the right people's experiences and, of course, involving the right people. We were paving new roads.

As willful as I am, I'm a strong believer in mentors. Mentorship is something we learned to harness after a few years of trying things on our own. It took too long to start from scratch and reinvent the wheel. At first, we maintained our independence and did things ourselves. Soon we realized we could grow much faster by being a sponge to new ideas from people with vastly different experiences than our own. By casting a wide net for mentors with expertise in different functional areas, we were able to choose what felt relevant and leave behind anything that wasn't. Access to this knowledge was invaluable.

I focused on finding mentors for things such as organizational structure, human resource processes, compensation, budgeting, and several other functions. In doing so, I started building a network of skill-based mentors. Unity's mentors helped the team develop processes, facilitate planning, give advice, donate services, share resources, and open doors. We identified where we needed help, found the right mentors, co-created plans to level up, and did the work to fill gaps.

When people felt valued and heard that their contribution was tangible and impactful, they often gave more. Eventually our grant writer, Malik, found a group called Social Venture Partners Toronto (SVP Toronto) that donated consulting time to one organization for three years. We had to compete with over forty charities to be considered for support from SVP Toronto. The process was intense. We did an interview after submitting an application and then presented at the McKinsey & Company office in front of hundreds of consultants. Finally, we got the good news: we were chosen to receive support for three years of free consulting; we utilized this support to the fullest.

I discovered later that compared to the other organizations SVP Toronto supported, Unity took advantage of drastically more hours of free consulting time. Other organizations supported by SVP Toronto the same year as Unity received three hundred to four hundred hours of pro bono consulting on an annual basis. Unity had been provided with over fourteen hundred hours of consulting in one year with nearly thirty consultants. In other words, we took *full* advantage of this opportunity, meeting with consultants early in the morning and late in the evening nearly every day for almost three years. I remember even meeting with consultants on weekends and holidays just to get through some of our work. It was like bringing Tupperware containers to an all-you-can eat buffet. All of these hours with consultants helped to build Unity in key times of growth.

Every evolutionary stage of Unity required different types of support. At first we were just building within our means. We brought together artists, volunteers, and community to build our programs. Once we began to focus on growth, we started bringing in mentors to help craft different processes and teach us different ways of operating an organization. When we got that stuff locked down, we started growing and fundraising and creating strategy that we began to execute in our own unique way. Each stage of Unity's evolution required different types of mentors. From start-up (entrepreneurs) to growth (strategic thinkers) to maintenance (governance specialists) to succession (management consultants and recruiters).

We eventually began to internalize this mentorship by recruiting a well-balanced board of directors with skills in key functional areas. This network of mentors became champions of our cause and in many cases donors as well.

For me, every role within an organization has a life cycle. This includes the leader, the board, and the team. New blood brings new expertise and new thinking and can be vital to the organization for its growth and evolution. We were fortunate to have had several amazing board chairs at the forefront of leadership for Unity. One of our board members, Shane Green, said it was like the movie *The Godfather*. We needed to have the right consigliere for the right time.

Consigliere directly translates to *advisor* from Italian. The right advisors. Each board member at Unity brought with them valuable experience and new perspectives that supported us through the various pressure points of our growth. A well-managed and constantly evolving board was one of Unity's key success factors.

Unity's first board chair was Josh Singer, whom I met in high school. Josh brought an entrepreneurial focus, and he taught me to set big goals and create work-back schedules to achieve those goals. On his terms, Josh grew his startup into one of the top Canadian companies. Together we were both building something out of nothing. He was the perfect startup chair to lead our first board.

Next came Eric Goldstrand. Eric is the vice-president of a major finance company that focuses on long-term investments. As the board chair, he brought strategic thinking and razor-sharp focus. He taught me the value of strategy and how to really think through ideas before executing, and he had a critical eye for issues and real experience in big business situations to back it up. He brought grounded and thoughtful leadership to the board: he didn't speak too often, but when he did, he had something profound to share that often shifted our thinking. Eric taught me the importance of thinking before speaking and being critical in order to learn and grow. He always used to tell me, "No one cares how much you know until they know how much you care."

The next chair was Azim Alibhai. Azim helped cowrite Unity's mission statement and was a big mentor to me personally. As we were scaling our programs, he brought in something so important: he reminded us of where we came from, our roots. He always focused on mission and impact with heartfelt sincerity and kindness. He reaffirmed the focus on people in the organization and the importance of adhering to our values. He reminded me constantly of the importance of putting the youth first in every decision and often brought up the full circle that Unity enabled for youth who came back as alumni, mentors, artist educators, and staff. Azim did my first performance review and taught me critical areas I needed to focus on to grow as a leader. He told bad dad jokes at the beginning of every meeting, but I would not trade his contribution for anything.

Next was Adam Silver. Adam is one of the most thoughtful management consultants and recruiters I have ever known. I met Adam as part of SVP Toronto, where he was a consultant on Unity's projects. He did our final project with SVP Toronto to restructure our board, and then he left SVP to be able to join our board and became a vital mentor to me. He offered an incredibly strategic thought process, challenged me often, and helped me with many of the issues we faced. Generally, when we wanted to meet someone in the business world, Adam somehow knew them. He gave strategic guidance but never interfered with operational decisions. He was a genuine supporter to me when I was dealing with my succession and at the peak of my anxiety. I am so thankful to have had him as chair during this time.

Each board chair had a dedicated group of board members around the table who made the success possible: from bank presidents to HR professionals to school teachers to youth alumni. The board's evolution was in line with the organization's needs at particular times in its evolution. We really brought in the right consigliere for the right time. I am so thankful to our board members as friends, mentors, and bosses.

BUILD REFLECTION QUESTIONS

Reflect on the plane (a.k.a. the idea) that you are building while flying.

1. What are you building? If you are not yet at the building stage, what ideas are you thinking of building?
2. What need or problem does your idea aim to address? How is your understanding of the need evolving as you build your plane?
3. Have you invited any mentors or stakeholders to the table? What specifically are you seeking to learn or gain from external expertise?
4. What are you learning as you build your plane? (Tip: consider failures lessons!)
5. How are you prioritizing where you spend your time? What is the most urgent thing you need to focus on? What is the most critical thing you need to focus on? How do you differentiate between things that are urgent and things that are critical?
6. What are your "chicken and eggs" of growth? (For example, trying to pay people despite having few resources.)
7. What resources do you need in the coming year to build your plane effectively?

    a. Create a budget to identify resources required to effectively execute your idea.
    b. Consider scenarios: optimistic, realistic, by month/quarter/year, by program. (Refer to "Tools & Resources" at the end of the book for templates.)
    c. What non-financial resources does your building process require? (Examples: in-kind product/service, access to networks, knowledge, expertise, mentors. Keep in mind that great ideas are often built and tested with volunteers.)

8. What pressure points are you experiencing that indicate you may need to learn something new or grow your organization? (Example: Staff capacity is at its limit with four programs, but you plan to launch another program within the next thirty days.)

9. What small "bricks" can you lay to build the foundation today for your idea? (Examples: apply for your first grant, co-create a mission statement, choose a form of registration.)

PART 3

TRUST
Crews and Cyphers

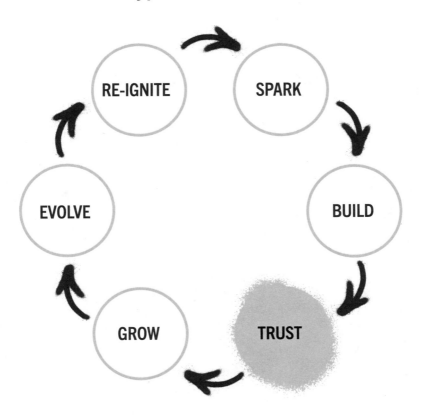

One of the most powerful things about breakin' to me is my crew. A crew is a group of people you roll with. You practise with your crew, you hang with your crew, you battle with your crew, you party with your crew — and you hold each other accountable. My crew are my brothers and sisters through thick and thin. When my parents were splitting up and my mom was battling schizophrenia, I'd hang with my crew. They were my second family.

It is the contributions of the individual to a big vision that create a crew. Within crews there is a certain vibe, one that forms and evolves based on the talents and strengths of everyone involved. We practise together and push each member to be better, while paying attention to who is improving, who needs support, and watch for those who are ready to represent the crew in battle.

With my crew, we battled based on our individual strengths and how these strengths are exponentially enhanced together. It was almost like a group of superheroes, all with alter egos, just making sense of our gifts in a cohesive way. Instead of having top-down leadership, we focused on the power we harnessed collectively and shared a strong set of values that held us together. Our experience together went far beyond the dance.

BREAKIN': CREW LEADERSHIP

A crew shares a powerful bond. My crew has my back and I've got theirs. While we come from very different cultural backgrounds, we share a common way of looking at the world. A way of seeing this dance. A way of treating people. It's an unsaid code. It's a language. You just know. When someone walks like you, carries themselves with the same integrity, this is crew. There is no stronger bond and support network than my crew.

When I started Unity, I saw the team as another crew. The prospect of being a boss was foreign to me. I loved harnessing the ideas of large groups and finding a collective direction, but I didn't like making decisions without the input of others.

Just like a crew, Unity had its code of values. We told people that when they wore a Unity t-shirt with our logo on it they had to live our values of respect, passion, integrity, youth, and community. This statement and our adherence to it helped us launch a line of clothing with big Unity logos in bright colours. Artists, staff, and youth in our programs wore these shirts with pride as a reminder to live with Unity's values. Anyone can get outfitted at Unity Shop, and people literally wore our values on their chest. Two young people, Andrew Trac and Branden Taylor, believed so much in Unity's values that they even got a Unity tattoo. Unity's values spoke to how we worked together — they were more than just a corporate statement. We even had a secret handshake for those who were part of the Unity crew that we taught to staff, artists, volunteers, youth, and even board members. We would facilitate discussions years after they were created, telling stories about how we were living Unity's values out in the world, a reminder that they were relevant and being practised.

"CREW LEADERSHIP" IN ACTION

LEADERSHIP POLARITIES

empowerment
delegation
contribution

accountability
clarity
decision making

TRUST HOLDS IT TOGETHER

BREAKIN': THE CODE OF THE CYPHER

The cypher is a key part of breakin' and how we communicate, learn, and grow. It is a proving ground to test ideas and receive instant feedback. A cypher happens in the form of a circle so you can see everyone you are sharing the space with. Each dancer goes in the centre one at a time to share. A good cypher is like a strong team: individuals come together to create something that could not have been achieved in isolation. You push each other to be better. Cyphers are opportunities to exchange unique perspectives while listening and holding space for others to share their ideas with respect. Some cyphers have a focus towards "power moves," some on "top rocks" (dancing that is done standing up), and some focus on "footwork." Like an effective team, people in a cypher need to pay attention to their environment and be ready to adapt.

Cyphers are transformational spaces for growth and development. You are celebrated for stepping out of your comfort zone and sharing your unique style. Instant recognition encourages people to take chances. People can redefine themselves in a single moment in the cypher. Someone who is usually shy can share another part of themselves; we bring new parts of ourselves that no one sees outside of the cypher. It's a place to build inner confidence by being acknowledged for your unique talents. Imagine what would happen if we created cyphers in the workplace and celebrated people for expressing their individuality. At Unity we tried to create spaces for employees to feel safe to be themselves and contribute. Trying out innovative ideas was encouraged just as it is in the cypher, whether you succeed or not.

You need to listen to know how to best respond in the cypher. The cypher teaches dancers to better understand their environment. There is a language, an unsaid code, that one must learn. For example, it is important you don't step on each other when jumping in. Also, if you see an elder stepping into the cypher and they look like they are going to dance, it is understood you give them the space in the centre. It's a sign of respect. Just like in building an organization, we need to learn the unspoken protocols of the ecosystem we work in through experience. In everything from government fundraising to building a high-functioning board of directors, we learn through doing by jumping into the cypher, trying out ideas and adapting. Cyphers are also spaces to have constructive conversations. You can safely challenge people and call them out if you want to test their skills. This is a respectful way to push someone you want to help grow.

The cypher is a transformational space for innovation, team building, and learning. How can we create safe spaces to test new ideas at work, challenge each other respectfully, and celebrate our teams for their unique contributions? How can we create "cyphers" at work? Give respect, celebrate individuality, show and prove, learn by doing, and explore strengths we didn't know we even had.

I NEVER WANTED TO BE A BOSS

So you can imagine, because I was fifteen years old when I started Unity, I never saw myself as a boss. I saw the team as another crew of contributors who led from our values. Unity needed leadership, but did it need a traditional boss? The prospect of being the boss disturbed me. I've always been good at gathering people's ideas and pulling them together to take action, but what I've never liked is having to make decisions on everyone's behalf.

I often had funny moments where people didn't know I was in charge. One day the building's caretaker came up to me in the hallway and said, "Is your boss doing good?"

I paused for a moment, not really sure how to reply. I said, "Yup, he's great." Then I slowly realized he thought Mike Thomas, Unity's director of operations, was my boss because he was in his forties and sometimes wore dress shirts. When Mike left Unity, the caretaker found out and asked if I'd be taking his job. At this point I had to break the news to him that I was technically in charge, even though I didn't always act like it. He laughed and walked away. I guess because I wear sweatpants, silly animal t-shirts, and sneakers at work, people assume I'm not responsible or just a kid. I learned from my dad to fully be yourself and people will align with you, your true being, who you *really* are. People also let their guard down a bit when they think I'm just some kid. I'm not out to impress anyone or create slick first impressions. If people don't accept me for who I am, then it is likely a sign that our values don't align and that's completely okay.

It didn't take long for my team to see how much this idea of being a boss bothered me, so some of them started playfully calling me "boss" and then I would call them "boss" in rebuttal. I was bothered by the harmful power dynamics that this word brought to mind for me. "Boss" felt like a bad word, so I never used it. In meetings I would even randomly announce that our youngest staff member or someone who had recently impressed me on the team was now in charge of the organization, and then leave the room. For me, if staff earned my trust, it was something they would not break if they lived our values. Sometimes I got taken advantage of, but my trust more often led to great results. When people asked me why our culture was so strong, I pointed to our unflinching, almost dangerous, levels of trust: Trust that put staff and artists in the driver's seat. Trust that gave people the space to fail. Trust that made the team feel like a crew.

Boss or not, being at the top affected my health. I don't know how other leaders manage. I remember over the years of growing Unity I would go home at least once a week and ask my wife, Mel, "Why the hell am I doing this to myself? No one should feel this terrible doing something they love so much." Honestly, I don't think being a leader of an organization, taking on the full weight of responsibility, is healthy. I wouldn't wish this level of stress on my worst enemy . . . but it also felt strangely worth it. I saw the impact we had on the communities we served, even while I saw the impact Unity was having on my health. The sacrifices were real, and I faced a constant polarization between my passion for this work and the stress that it caused.

Deep down, I dreamed of not being in the lead role, especially when the weight of it began to impact my psyche. As resilient as I had learned to become in my personal life, it was different leading Unity. I was able to take charge, but I really didn't like it. I didn't like being an authority figure over anyone else in the decision-making process. It was conflicting for me. I didn't believe in making decisions without input from the team and community. I asked for people's opinions and listened carefully. I engaged people so often that sometimes they even wanted me to just decide and stop asking them for their opinion.

Despite resisting the power dynamics in the hierarchy, I accepted that it was the best option to move things forward in an organized way. We utilized the hierarchy with a crew mentality to move the mission forward. We found resilience in striking a balance, in working within a hierarchy even though I did not believe in a top-down approach. I tried to lead as democratically as I could. And I still truly believed that the team and artists were running Unity collectively.

We also had to work through the challenges that my lenient approach to management enabled. I gave people the space to dream, but this was sometimes too much space and enabled people to get away with a lot. On a positive note, what it did do was allow work to feel less oppressive, to have work be a psychologically safer place where people's unique contributions were valued. For some this presented a lack of clarity, accountability, and decision-making. But people learned to work in this environment. Opportunities arose that could never have been possible in a more command-and-control style environment. I wanted to create a space where people could be themselves at work while still getting shit done.

I would go home stressed out, but I'd return to work the next day and this feeling would go away, because no matter how much I dreaded firing people, fundraising, or dealing with Canada Revenue Agency, seeing our team truly empowered and the impact we were having kept me going. It fuelled me, while at the same time the stress was draining the tank.

We were able to provide real jobs for people within the hip hop community. For us, this was a huge achievement, as members of this community often experience precarious employment or are forced to take multiple jobs just to make rent. We were able to provide artists with jobs they loved and were passionate about, and pay them above industry standard. In some ways this was my own personal second mission for the organization. I was motivated by something greater, even though I felt terrible inside. It was a dangerous cycle. I was hurting myself to help others.

Flipping Culture: Everyone Takes out the Trash

As I said at the top when I spoke about the importance of crew, I'm a strong believer that every person has the right to be valued and treated with respect, no matter their title, role, or experience. In my view, hierarchies affect the way we look at ourselves and the way others look at us, and they can be oppressive on an institutional level if the power is mishandled. I really believe that my opinion is not any more valuable than anyone else's. But, in spite of my views on a hierarchical structure, we still had to find ways to come to decisions as an organization. If you work for Unity, no matter your position, you are important and treated with respect. It took a ton of work to infuse the crew mentality in Unity's hierarchy to support the team to lean into strengths, strive for learnings, and bring more of themselves to work. It took time and was frustrating for some of the team, but I believe it was worth it.

We built a culture at Unity where we all took out the trash, especially me. Even when we had enough funding to hire an office support staff who became responsible for taking out the trash, I still made sure that I took it out, showing my staff that no one is too senior for any task that contributes to our mission. Also, it's just the right thing to do.

UNITY'S TEAM MODEL: FLATTENING THE HIERARCHY

This Venn diagram shows how each member of the team is critical to achieving Unity's goals as an organization. It shows that even though teams have different focus areas (operations or leadership), we offer all

TEAM MODEL

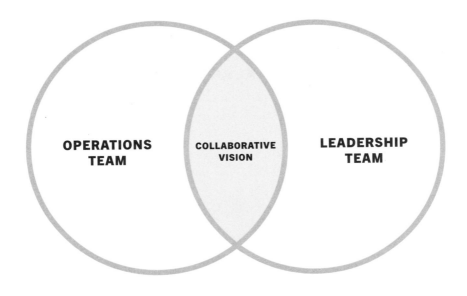

OPERATIONS
TEAM

COLLABORATIVE
VISION

LEADERSHIP
TEAM

staff opportunities to collaborate and contribute. Everyone is given the space to contribute new ideas, visions, and dreams.

Unity's leadership team's key responsibility is to ensure the strategic plan is being followed across the entire organization and across all members of the team. The operations team is responsible for executing Unity programs and key functions within the organization to allow those programs to be possible.

There is a critical overlap between the teams: collaboration and collective visioning. The leadership team needs to be involved in implementation by supporting and collaborating with the operations team, as well as executing at times. Everyone needs to remain grounded and connected. The operations team is encouraged to give input on Unity's strategy and tactics by providing input on the effectiveness of current strategies or presenting new ideas. The key is each side of the team focuses on their key area, but they are constantly collaborating with and showing respect for ideas from the other stakeholders. Ultimately, everyone is given an opportunity to contribute.

LEADING WITH VULNERABILITY: SHARING STORIES TO HEAL AND CONNECT

There is a sensitive dance between sharing your story and taking advantage of those you serve for the purposes of fundraising. I've heard so many times that "if it bleeds, it reads," and people have told me to create moments that "pull on donors' heart strings." I fundamentally disagree with this idea. Many charities seeking donations aim to share a story that says "your program changed someone's life"; however, things are not that simple. It's vital that any person who shares their story is proud of it in the moment and proud of it after it is shared. Our goal at Unity was to empower people who felt ready to share their story in their own words.

We did not script stories. We had everyone from youth alumni to artists to funders to school administrators to staff share their stories to connect and engage with students, faculty, donors, and community partners. We took this responsibility very seriously, addressing everything from confidentiality to trigger warnings to consent.

Trauma is complex. We never know when we tell our stories if they might re-traumatize us or someone who is hearing our story in the process of just remembering or sharing difficult events. Storytelling is a powerful form of communication. This is why Unity tried to focus on stories of empowerment, overcoming, success, and growth. Unity always told its storytellers that they could share as much or as little as they wish. This had to be said, as people might have assumed we wanted them to share a tough, heart-wrenching story to pull at funders' heartstrings and help raise money. Pressuring people to use the hardship and trauma as a way to raise money, I believe, is immoral.

Unity's goal was to create empowering story-sharing experiences for everyone involved. When done well, stories can have a transformational positive impact and be very healing. Still, this was a sensitive balancing act, and we believed that anyone asking someone to share their story must be willing to lead by example. As someone in a position of authority, I wanted to exemplify these values. Know what it feels like yourself before asking someone else to share. Being open and vulnerable helps set the stage for others. Have you ever been to a wedding when one person starts crying and then a wave of others begins to cry out of joy? I see the same thing happen with storytelling in the right environment and context. We have to set the stage for safer storytelling environments.

Unfortunately, we learned about storytelling in the wrong context the hard way. Unity trained its artist educators to share their stories in programs to heal, engage, and connect with youth. At the end of an out-of-town program, we had a major sponsor performance. We invited youth from high schools we worked with that week to perform and share their stories. Several hours before the show, our artists worked with the youth to practise sharing their stories.

In the middle of the show, one of the youth shared their story, but this time, they shared a different one than they had rehearsed. They talked for over ten minutes about a traumatic event they had experienced, in vivid and extremely explicit detail. This was happening in front of the staff of one of Unity's biggest sponsors, who had brought their young children to watch. I remember crying backstage. I was petrified for everyone involved. My number one goal was to ensure the safety of the young person sharing.

After a quick and intense deliberation backstage, we allowed the young person to finish without interruption. It felt like they had finally felt safe to share this; they just needed to let it out — even though it was an audience that was not ready for what was being told. When they got off stage, we gave them a ton of support and made sure to get their contact information and inform their school. For years we followed up with this young person's school principal to ensure they were safe.

It didn't end there. We had angry sponsors sending us emails about how we had traumatized their young children by exposing them to these stories. We sent personalized follow-up apology letters to each employee. I felt sick to my stomach. I had never been so certain in my life as I was in that moment that Unity was finished. Thankfully, almost everyone ultimately understood that this was a powerful and important moment for this young person: for the first time in their life they had felt safe enough to share this experience. I will never forget this day.

This experience taught us that we needed to add new protocol for sharing our stories, and we spent a ton of time and energy to create safer spaces for youth and artists to open up. We created a process that was part of Unity's artist training retreat to allow our artist educators to share their stories amongst peers, often for the first time, in a structured way. This was a three-day retreat in the wilderness, getting people away from their usual patterns and day-to-day experience. Throughout this retreat, we coached artists to safely and powerfully share their stories. The goal was a process of healing, support, and empowerment. The retreat also focused on building other key skills on becoming an effective artist educator.

The Unity team created a short checklist of ideas to consider in preparing to share our stories. We encouraged artists not to share anything they were not ready to share. This was very important. Personal stories can have a powerful role in the healing process and engaging youth, but they can also trigger traumatic memories. It was critical that we create a supportive environment to facilitate this process for Unity's artist educators. Artists decided what and how much they wanted to share. It was all about context. We facilitated a process to harness the power of sharing their stories in programs while safeguarding themselves.

We started with a writing reflection, including a series of questions to help artists write out the parts of their story they find to be relevant to share with youth in the programs. Beginning the storytelling process this way gave some space to individually explore experiences and raw ideas before sharing them. It can be hard to gauge what feels right to share, so we had a few experienced artist educators share their stories first to set the stage. This usually took a full day of our retreat. It was important that the activity had time to breathe. We ensured there was no time limit on this section. After writing our stories, we broke into small groups spread out in the wilderness or wherever the artists felt most comfortable, and gave them the opportunity to select parts to share. This allowed them to break down small stories they felt ready to share and get feedback from an experienced Unity facilitator.

We encouraged artists to support each other and celebrate bravery while they explored stories they thought might be relevant to youth in high school. Artists shared moments of empowerment, overcoming adversity through hip hop, and key challenges they worked through. Everyone has a story. We celebrated anyone for sharing their truth. Acknowledgement, support, and encouragement were critical throughout this process. Stories unfolded through this facilitated exploration filled with tears, hugs, and laughter. The storytelling portion of the retreat happened once the group had built some trust, usually by the last full day together. This provided a testing ground to explore stories of empowerment while articulating the purpose of sharing in connection to Unity's mission. Between 2010 and 2018, Unity ran fifteen separate artist training retreats across Canada led mostly by Testament, RaSoul, Andel James, Cat, and Jessey Pacho. I participated in every single one. Openly sharing my story throughout Unity's evolution helped me to lead by example and build a culture of trust, vulnerability, and honesty amongst our community of artists, board, staff, and youth.

When we share something about a challenging moment, we may be triggering other people who hear our story; people who have experienced other forms of trauma. At Unity, we encouraged those sharing their stories to use trigger warnings to let people know in advance if something they plan to share may be triggering to others; for example, "I'm about to share a story that references abusive relationships. If this might be triggering for you, feel free to walk out and grab a breath of fresh air. Our team is here to talk with you after the show if you need extra support or an ear to listen."

We tried to be conscious when we were asking someone who is comfortable sharing their story to not push them to share it over and over. Even when people are empowered in their stories, the repetition of telling can become problematic. We always treated story sharing as though it was the first time, preparing ourselves and others to share, asking permission and letting people know they can back out at any point. Because we realized the power story sharing had to allow people to heal and connect, we approached from a place of empowerment, but also one of consent and agency. Safety was our number-one priority.

At Unity, we always let people know not to share things they are not ready to talk about. We weren't there to give people advice or tell them how to live their lives. We were just sharing our experiences. Counselling and giving advice are the jobs of child and youth workers, social workers, and psychologists. We were just there to share and listen. Sharing our stories became a powerful tool for Unity artist educators to break down barriers and build stronger relationships when working with youth. Still, storytelling is complex and should be approached with respect and careful consideration. Before going down this path and opening the possible floodgates, we need to really reflect. Once we open the tap, we need to be prepared to navigate the water.

SELF-CARE IS CONTAGIOUS

Among staff at Unity, there didn't seem to be a healthy separation between work life and home life, as the passion for the work bubbled over. Work was life. This took a real toll on people's mental and physical health, mine included. It took some deep reflection for me to understand that work is a big part of our life, but not all of our life. My failure as a leader was that I was hurting everyone who looked up to me on my team, setting a negative example by not taking care of myself.

I used to send emails as soon as an idea popped into my head. Midnight, 2:00 a.m., 4:00 a.m., it didn't matter. I would wake up and send it. I would also send emails on evenings, weekends, and holidays. I was an email machine! In ten years at Unity I sent 426,808 emails (that averages to 116 emails per day over ten years)! Sometimes I felt the more emails I sent, the more successful Unity would be. But what this told my team was that it was okay and, maybe in some cases, might even be expected. I only realized this wasn't okay when one of my teammates, Rajni Sharma, mentioned it. I broke myself of the habit, and it became the first step in encouraging the separation of work and home, for me personally and as a part of Unity's culture. I set time restrictions on when I would send emails, schedule meetings, and answer phone calls. Like a crew, we looked out for one another and could call each other out when we could see someone falling into unhealthy patterns. Obviously, sometimes we had to keep working and emailing through crunch periods, but overall we tried to develop a more self-aware and self-care approach to work-life balance. It was an ongoing grind, but it was worth it.

I began dancing more and meditating during this time. As I created a culture of care for myself, I noticed that this created space for staff to develop their own self-care practices. It had always been encouraged, but actions spoke louder than words. Staff collectively began taking breaks in the middle of the workday to go to the gym. They were holding each other accountable. I look at the power of my influence anytime I am "in charge" of something as a responsibility to lead by example; so I worked on creating the best possible work environment by treating myself well while I was encouraging others to do the same for themselves. It was so simple, but not so obvious. Saying "take care of yourself" was meaningless without leadership that modelled the behaviour.

I want people to know that you don't need to kill your minds and bodies to be successful or to feel that through your own sacrifice, someone else will benefit. I think that's a sad and shitty story we tell ourselves. I told myself this story for nearly a decade before I decided to make a change. We need to work intelligently and efficiently. If I don't sleep, my employees ultimately won't sleep because I've normalized and enabled this behaviour. It's not okay, and I needed to be the one who set the example by practising what I preach.

There were times where I would break my own rules, but I would try to acknowledge it in front of others. We held each other accountable. This was hard work to turn off, and when big deadlines were in our face we needed to perform and kill it. Just acknowledging busy times could make it feel like we were in it together. It allowed people to take care of each other during the process and gave space for them to take time off afterward. Self-care became contagious.

> I realized that if I want the team to have loyalty to and respect for the organization, I needed to have respect for myself. We gave our employees full-time, permanent jobs, even when the world is moving towards temporary contract work, to show we respected and valued them. Over time, we were able to provide staff with health, dental, and mental health benefits, laptops, transportation support, and phones. We even began to give annual bonuses and on-the-spot gift card bonuses as incentives for above-and-beyond performance. It required real investment in our people. People in power need to make conscious efforts rooted in real intentions to build a healthier work environment. It's vital to the well-being of future generations of work. It's just the right thing to do. Ultimately, taking care of our people helped all of Unity's bottom lines, from team culture to staff retention to program impact to funds raised and beyond.

It was critical to me to unite the team towards a shared direction and get them to take ownership of their contributions. People personally invested in our programs, each one created by an individual stemming from their knowledge, passion, and vision for their specific area of the organization. For example, Cat built Community Programs as one of the best hip hop dancers in the country; Rajni built the festival from her passion for art therapy; Mahad Shoaib built an evaluation process after being a participant in the Unity programs; and Diamond Osoteo built our bookings social enterprise from his past experiences supporting emerging artists across the city. Together the team built Unity from the ground up, fuelled by their passion and authentic connection to the community.

Every action was connected to the big picture. One of our core philosophies was to do what's best for Unity and the youth, not our egos, not our jobs, not our own interests. By holding ourselves to this, the team was united and invested in the impact we were having. This included me. It also applied to board members. At informal interviews with potential board members, at some point in the meeting we would listen for something along the lines of, "I don't want to get in the way. All I want to do is help. If I'm not of value to the board, don't let me take up a seat." It was the secret password to join the Unity board. It told us a lot. We knew their ego would be checked at the door. We needed to be able to challenge each other respectfully and with the best interest of the cause.

The mission was at the centre of every decision and action. I created a process to acknowledge our distance from the centre. I like to draw, so I drew a circle made up of concentric rings. I labelled the circle in the middle *Youth*. Youth was literally the reason the organization existed, so it was placed in the centre of this diagram. The frontline artist educators were the closest to the youth, so the first ring out from the centre represented them. Then came a ring representing program coordinators who supervised, managed, and trained frontline artists. The next layer out represented the staff who contributed behind the scenes by performing fundraising, finance, and office functions. The next layer out from that was the board of directors who managed risk and created a governance structure in support of the entire organization.

The reason I regularly brought this to the team's attention was that youth had to be at the centre of everything we did, and we could never lose sight of that. It was a reminder that if you were on one of the outer rings based on the nature of your role and not interacting with our beneficiaries on a daily basis, you needed to constantly check in to programs and realign yourself with our core purpose. It was vital that staff at all levels felt and experienced the impact, especially when they perceived themselves as disconnected from the centre, so they could make sound decisions in best service to the mission and the youth. It is easy to make decisions on behalf of others, but our vision was to integrate youth voices at every stage possible, and this took extra work, especially for those farthest from the centre. This enabled an adaptive and responsive organization that genuinely listened and responded to youth.

It wasn't always easy to know if we had a positive impact on the youth we served. To better understand our impact, we created an evaluations committee made up of representatives from our board of directors, staff, and youth. This put accountability on Unity's leadership and programs team to measure and understand the program outcomes. We also tried to make sure the evaluation process was ethical and useful to youth we served.

To this end, we invested in a nearly year-long process to create what is known as a theory of change with the help of Innoweave, who gave us funding to hire an incredible consultant, Robin Cory. Robin worked with our leadership team and board to create this tool to help define Unity's

A YOUTH-CENTRED ORGANIZATION

YOUTH ARE THE CORE OF WHAT WE DO. ALL DECISIONS MUST INVOLVE YOUTH. IF STAFF ARE ON THE OUTER RINGS WE MUST CONNECT WITH OUR CENTRE AND OUR CORE, THE YOUTH.

DIRECTORS
& EXECUTIVES

COORDINATORS

YOUTH

ARTISTS

VOLUNTEERS

impact. A theory of change is a participatory planning and evaluation tool that helps non-profits map out big goals. It helps teams agree upon and better understand the conditions required to achieve their intended impact. How can we hold ourselves accountable for long-term outcomes in a program where impact is very hard to measure? What claims are we comfortable signing our names to? We wanted to push for big impact while still remaining grounded in reality. Inaccurate and unchallenged assumptions could lead us astray. The theory of change process helped us understand our impact through challenging the truth of what we took for granted.

We had to set a clear yardstick of what success looked like, not just on an output level but an outcome level as well. We landed on output metrics of attendance and retention. If youth weren't showing up, it told us to dig deeper. Maybe the program was not engaging, maybe the program was not in an easy-to-access location, maybe the facilitators hired an artist that needed more training. The numbers spoke volumes, but sometimes there was a natural barrier to us achieving our planned outputs that we could not control, like a snowstorm on the day of the final student showcase.

We also chose outcome metrics related to mental health. We were aiming to build youth resilience through strengthening individual protective factors. Through this process we learned that "protective factors buffer a person in the face of adversity and moderate the impact of stress on social and emotional well-being, thereby reducing the likelihood that disorders will develop."[1] Protective factors may be internal (e.g., temperament, cognitive abilities) or external (e.g., social, economic, or environmental supports). They enable a person to protect their emotional and social well-being and cope with everyday life events

---

1   World Health Organization, "Promotion, Prevention and Early Intervention for Mental Health: A Monograph," Commonwealth Department of Health and Aged Care (2000): 13

(whether positive or negative). Protective factors act as a buffer against stress and may be drawn upon in dealing with stressful situations.[2] We began to ground our work in research around mental health, resilience, and protective factors.

What can responsible impact look like for Unity? This is what the process of creating a theory of change did for us. It was a framework for defining our impact. It was literally the theory of the change we strived to make through the work we did as an organization. It was our intended impact. It helped us define our short-term and long-term outcomes while defining inputs, activities, target beneficiaries, and metrics. It made us get specific and ask ourselves why we were making certain choices. The theory of change gave us a map, and the metrics became our compass to let us know if we were on track. This model helped us fly the plane in the right direction and cross-check to ensure we stayed on course. We were testing our impact theories in real time. The process was a significant time investment from the leadership team and board members, doing the homework to validate our assumptions about what was working. It engaged a wide variety of stakeholders and gave them a real voice in the final product. We co-created Unity's future, and although painful, it was worth it. If you would like to see Unity's theory of change, it can be found at epicleadership.ca/bookresources.

With our compass in place, we became more disciplined about saying no. Prior to launching new projects, we asked ourselves:

2   Centre for Addiction and Mental Health, with Dalla Lana School of Public Health University of Toronto, and Toronto Public Health, "Best practice guidelines for mental health promotion programs: Children (7–12) & youth (13–19)," CAMH Publications (2014): https://www.porticonetwork.ca/documents/81358/128451/Best+Practice+Guidelines+for+Mental+Health+Promotion+Programs+-+Children+and+Youth/b5edba6a-4a11-4197-8668-42d89908b606

1. Do we have the financial support for this? (Is someone willing to pay for it?)
2. Does our team have the capacity, bandwidth, or person power to do this?
3. Is it on-mission or in line with our ultimate impact goals as an organization?

This process allowed our team to stay on track and not become distracted or commit resources to tangential efforts.

For example, we deliberately did not apply for Canada 150 funding, available for projects celebrating Canada's sesquicentennial, even though many of our peers were doing so. For us, it was an obvious distraction. It was a large amount of short-term project funding, and it wasn't in line with our direction and mission. It would have taken us away from our theory of change. We could have made up a project idea that would likely have fit their mandate and allowed us access to a large amount of funding, but to Unity, this was irresponsible. Sustainability and saying no became a big part of every new program discussion.

We held ourselves accountable. Each staff member was responsible for setting individual, departmental, and collective goals against which we could measure ourselves. To us, evaluation was a compass, not a mine detector. It was about ensuring we were moving in the right direction and taking a holistic approach to working with youth. Sometimes targeting a potentially impactful project that is too specific might jeopardize the big-picture goal of building resilience in the youth we served. It's about balance. Not too specific, not too broad. The compass.

By being too specific we could potentially cause harm by cutting out some of the good stuff around the edges that is hard to measure. Sometimes critical impact happened at the periphery. We trusted our coordinators and frontline artists, who were outstanding youth workers, to be experts in building meaningful relationships with youth participants to support their development. The artists and staff co-developed the big-picture goals for the organization while applying their own style to implementing flexible roadmaps to get there. Style is very important in hip hop, and we embraced this in our programming, each individual expressing an idea through their strengths and creative approach. There are many ways to win a battle: we embraced individual style as we do in hip hop and followed the theory of change as our compass.

HIRE PEOPLE WITH DREAMS

I almost never look at someone's job experience when they apply for a position. I want to understand what people are capable of, not necessarily what they did in the past. I rarely want to know their education levels or awards. Instead, the most important recruitment tool is to ask them what their dreams are. Their connection to the cause — what fuels their passion — is far more important to me than their IQ or education. People with direct experience as an artist or with community work, and not necessarily as a vocation, bring a deeper dimension to the team, and ultimately to the organization's success, because they can relate to it on a very intimate level. You can't go to school for what we do. You have to have lived it, breathed it, felt it.

My own story is connected to Unity from multiple angles, which is why it's so easy for me to talk about, sell, and authentically do what I do. It is a part of my story and the story of so many other artists and creatives on our team. You can't capture this feeling on a résumé. I had to experience their passion and challenge their commitment to know if they could add value to the Unity crew. I always told the staff and artists that they did not work for Unity — they were Unity.

We strived to build a team that embodied honesty, integrity, and drive. This beat any flashy résumé. Drive and desire to learn are what matter most, not what school someone attended. I looked for people with resilience and who personally connected with the work. The few times I've broken this rule, ignoring the culture fit feeling, I've been disappointed with my hiring decision. Invested people create a strong culture. Strong culture enabled life-changing impact in our programs.

Flipping Hiring: Ditch the Résumé

Meeting people face-to-face for me is the only way to really tell if someone was a fit or not. There are too many things that can be missed skimming applications and holding phone interviews.

One of the most important factors in having what it took to be a great employee at Unity was having a personal connection to the work we did. Hip hop practically saved my life. This made my job far more than just work for me, and it was, in many ways, connected to my purpose in life. Because our work often connected to parts of each staff's purpose and passion, Unity became an ideal environment in which to build culture and commitment. People's personal connections to Unity were often in relation to hip hop, being part of an artistic community, being an artist, or having overcome adversity through art and community. Staff who saw a gap in their community often saw Unity as a platform to make a change. Some staff even had their own personal projects: Diamond Osoteo, for example, was Unity's bookings coordinator, and in his spare time created The Industry, an organization supporting emerging dancers. Ella Avila, Unity's finance and administration coordinator, created HER

Creative TO, an artistic showcase supporting top female talent. Even though people's independent projects were not part of Unity directly, the team would often support each other's initiatives.

When hiring, we were looking for staff with a direct tie to Unity's mission of serving youth through hip hop and arts-based programming. Some staff mentioned that they wished they had a program like Unity in their high school. Some outright told us about the direct connections, and some were even former participants in Unity programs. Sometimes it was hard to see personal connection through an interview process. Not everyone who worked at Unity had obvious personal connections or even connections that they spoke about. For some employees, I only learned after many years working at Unity what motivated them to do this work. There was almost always a powerful motivator beyond just a paycheque.

Our highest performing employees usually did not over-promise. They worked hard and proved themselves through their actions. Similar to the foundational values in hip hop, they showed and proved. It became part of the culture at Unity to be humble and show results.

Employees at Unity were eager to learn, grow, and develop their career and skills. People who cared about youth, and who had an "always learning" mentality, thrived at Unity. This was hard to identify in interviews. We added questions and assignments to our interview process to understand what connections interviewees had to the cause and why they wanted to work at Unity. One of the most telling questions for me in the interview was, "With all other commitments in your life, how long do you see yourself being at Unity in the worst-case and best-case scenarios?" The answer would often show who was deeply dedicated to this work beyond it being just a job. Sometimes people said what they thought we wanted to hear. Sometimes people were truly honest in this moment. It wasn't easy to tell. We listened for dreams and ambitions. We tended to give opportunities to those who were driven to work hard and continue to level up.

Jessey: Proving Doubters Wrong

One thing we prided ourselves in at Unity was that we had employees that stayed dedicated in an industry that was often seen as having a revolving door. Staff retention in the non-profit sector is a struggle given unpredictable finances from year to year. But the majority of our employees stayed with Unity at least four years, and some stayed as long as ten! People's desire to work at Unity was the key to our success. Our team was from vastly different backgrounds and experiences and this created a uniquely diverse culture at Unity. One powerful example of a Unity staff member that truly embodied our values and this "always learning" mentality was Jessey "Phade" Pacho.

I heard about Jessey back in 2009 when Unity was part of an assembly at John Fraser Secondary School. The assembly involved youth hip hop artists from the school, and Jessey and his best friend were producing a graffiti mural to go behind the performers. There was a teacher-champion at the school who engaged Jessey in our program through his art class. This teacher, Brett Boivin, was a huge catalyst for Unity's success at John Fraser. I never actually got to meet Jessey on that day, because in preparation for the assembly he had been suspended by the principal and could not participate.

Several years later, I saw an artist painting outdoors at an event in Mississauga. I tapped him on the shoulder and asked him if he would be interested in working with Unity as an artist educator and come to our artist training retreat. He took my card, but didn't seem too into it. At the time, I didn't know this was the same graffiti artist from John Fraser. Eventually Jessey attended Unity's artist training and joined the Unity artist educator roster on contract. Unity got booked to go back to John Fraser several years later, and in conversation with Jessey we connected the dots and realized he was that young person who had not been allowed to participate in the assembly several years back. We decided to have Jessey go back to his high school and lead the program.

As part of the assembly, Jessey shared his story in front of his entire high school. Jessey's teachers and the same principal who had suspended him attended the assembly. It was truly a full-circle moment where Jessey proved to them and to anyone who doubted him that he had talent and was capable of doing anything he set his mind to.

A few years later, we brought Jessey to Halifax on one of Unity's first-ever national programs; it was Jessey's first time on an airplane. He did a phenomenal job. He continued to grow as an artist and educator, and in managing multiple stakeholders. His potential seemed endless. Every time we gave him something new, he rose above and beyond expectations.

When we had a job opening for an after-school program coordinator, Jessey decided to apply. We weren't sure if he was ready in terms of the administrative side of things, but once again we gave him a shot. Jessey joined the Unity staff full-time in 2014, organizing and implementing Unity's after-school programs.

The youth in Jessey's programs looked up to him, they respected him. Jessey continued to push his potential working with teachers, principals, and administrators. After a few years of learning and excelling in this role, we decided to move him into a different role, running Unity's national programs. Jessey went on to run over 150 Unity Day programs in five provinces, managing a team of over thirty of Unity's top artists, and juggling dozens of community partners, schools, funders, and stakeholders. He continued to push his potential. He grew from a role as a youth participant to running one of Unity's most important national initiatives. I cared about Jessey's success and pushed him into roles that he wasn't completely comfortable with, but he rose to the occasion every time. Jessey became a critical voice in shaping the direction of Unity's national programs and holding Unity to a high standard in terms of program quality, arts education, and hip hop culture. Jessey is one of many incredible people at Unity, whom many did not believe in, but whom we invested in and advocated for — and he proved his doubters wrong.

A Stepping Stone for Career Development

Unity was often a stepping stone for people's careers. Do what you love, push your limits, and evolve. This was at the heart of our staff culture. How are you building the skills and supporting the career path of each staff member? Investing in people's careers also helped with staff retention.

Unity was a training ground for many people who went on to do bigger and better things with their careers. We celebrated this. Some went on to further their education, some moved on to bigger non-profit organizations, some followed their personal dreams and toured the world. I am always proud of people when they move on, no matter where they go. One of my favourite things to do is provide a reference for an awesome Unity staff member. I even cried once giving a job reference for one of our past employees, Mike Thomas, a.k.a. "Mike T," because of how much he had done for Unity and for me personally.

I shared with the person who had called for Mike T's reference that when my dad was admitted to hospital in critical condition the night before our biggest event of the year, Mike T cancelled plans with his extended family in order to step in for me. He never even told me he did this. I heard it from another member of my team. It spoke to his integrity, what he did when no one was looking in a moment of personal crisis. It wasn't for credit, but because he truly cared about me. I told the person who was listening to me that they must think I'm crazy for crying on a reference call.

I am so thankful to have met some of the most talented youth workers, artists, and authentic human beings through this work. Here are just a few examples of staff members for whom Unity was a stepping stone:

MALIK MUSLEH, Unity's first grant writer and director of development, who went to Osgoode Hall Law School after six years of helping set the foundation for Unity's fundraising;

KEVIN REIGH, Unity's development coordinator, who moved on to become a Program Manager at the Toronto Arts Council under Community Arts, who helped us raised hundreds of thousands of dollars in his time at Unity;

MIKE THOMAS, Unity's first director of operations, who went on to become the executive director of another charity and eventually to work in government;

ERIN ZIMERMAN, one of Unity's top artist educators, who worked in hundreds of Unity programs over a decade and ended up becoming an art teacher at a local high school.

There were dozens of staff, artists, and youth alumni that moved on to amazing careers after working at Unity. I look at career development as a key part of Unity's impact, even though it was not overtly stated in our mission. It built culture by showing we had each other's backs beyond the walls of the organization. I am so proud of our incredible team and will forever celebrate their success, development, and growth.

PLAN FOR GETTING HIT BY A BUS

Unity eventually reached a point where it *felt* like it could not exist without me. This was in large part a problem of my own making because although I hated to make decisions, I was involved in almost all of them. I believed I had to be involved in, and sign off on, every decision. People would often ask me, "What would happen to Unity if you got hit by a bus?" I didn't have a good answer.

In the early years of Unity, employees felt they needed my approval for even the smallest decisions because I was invested in every detail, no matter how small. We were in survival mode daily, and if we didn't raise the money fast enough people wouldn't have jobs. If programs failed, our reputation in the community could be burned. I feared people would eventually leave if we didn't start to pay them better. These stresses made me feel I needed to be involved in every decision. I couldn't let anything go wrong, but being involved in everything was stretching me thin.

What I didn't realize was that I was undermining my team — something everyone was afraid to tell me. There were times when they thought I should be less involved, but all of us got so used to me being there, that it felt like the right way. I was an intense micromanager, managing from a place of fear of something going wrong.

I used to get a copy of every email that every staff member received and sent. I used to review and revise every grant before it went out. I interviewed all new hires, and every time Unity ran a program in another city I had to be there. I cared so much about Unity's survival that I couldn't let even the smallest details go without a second set of eyes. My eyes. I attended every single program, went to every principals meeting, and pitched every funder.

Being this involved was taking a heavy toll on me physically and mentally, and this led to my anxiety coming back. I had to make a change, or I wouldn't survive this constant grind. When I started Unity, I had a mentor who told me I had to share my story in order to grow Unity. This worked when we were building, but not for growing or sustaining Unity. Once Unity began growing rapidly, being at the centre of every decision made it nearly impossible to remove myself. I needed to learn to delegate, but I didn't know how.

It took me ten years to wake up. I realized I needed to remove myself from day-to-day decision making and start to enable others to make their own choices and be accountable for the results. The ultimate challenge was to actually do this. One accountability at a time, I removed myself from the picture. I slowly but surely trusted the team to own their successes and their mistakes. I let them recruit their own people and manage teams on their own. It was not only about giving up decision-making power, but rather giving people full credit and celebrating their successes.

I gave Ella full credit and decision-making accountability in our finance department. This was very scary for me, considering the challenges we had faced in finance and accounting in the past.

I let Rajni own communications, sponsorships, and corporate fundraising. I eventually was only going in for pitches when she asked me to be there.

I let Jessey and Bob Veruela fully own the national program. They began to build and manage their own budgets of over three hundred thousand dollars.

In the beginning, I used my story to build Unity, when no one would give us the time of day and no one seemed to care about Unity as much as I did. After tons of discovery, reflection, and letting go, Unity was eventually ready to live on without me. The real growth for me was learning that not only did I not need to be at the centre, but it was healthier for my team and for me personally if I wasn't. It wasn't about me. It was about building sustainable impact. I needed to take a step back so others could truly step forward. Learning to let go was an ego check, but I began giving my team the credit and took a step back so others could shine. Unity wasn't mine, it was becoming a movement beyond me. The team took ownership of Unity as they slowly became more accountable for sustaining its success.

INCUBATE CREATIVITY

Unity was an intentional platform and vehicle to incubate the creative ideas of artists, staff, and youth through our collective vision. Staff development at Unity was about building internal experts from unique and diverse experiences and backgrounds. We utilized Unity as a platform. This was the magic. If Unity's vision aligned with an individual's personal vision and our current needs, we made magic. In other words, if we had the funding to hire someone in a particular area, we always looked for someone who could bring their personal values and approach to life to the job. As I often said, you don't work for Unity — you are Unity. We incubated creative passion in our people.

We worked hard to create a respectful culture, one where we challenged each other to grow and commit to improvement and learning.

Everyone brought something new, and the personal touch they brought to the organization through their life experience enabled us to create new ways of tackling big challenges. As long as they had a learning mentality, worked hard, were passionate about their work, and welcomed critical feedback, then anything was possible. Good risks are risks taken building a culture of amazing people.

There is dignity in risking it all on people: Bob, Diamond, Ella, Mahad, Cat, Adrian, Testament, Andel, and many more, were all staff who built their jobs from the ground up, helped build the plane while flying it, and brought in their own life experiences to help us reach our goals.

Diamond, who worked on artist training, did so with strengths stemming from his personal passion for artist development, and as an artist himself. He was personally invested in providing opportunities for emerging artists, and it aligned with Unity's mission.

Tafiya ran Unity's weekly drop-in breakin' program at the Art Gallery of Ontario (AGO). The floor at the AGO was amazing for breakin'. Tafiya had realized the space was serving two distinct audiences: one was a group of young people who were brand new to breakin' and wanted to learn the techniques, and the other was a group of more experienced dancers who just wanted a spot to practise. Instead of choosing to serve one over the other, Tafiya decided to serve both. No one told him to do this, he just did it. And it was genius.

Every week Tafiya would wait around thirty minutes until the room filled up. Sometimes there were more than fifty dancers in the room at once. Tafiya would stop the music for a few moments and tell everyone, "If you want to learn what I'm teaching today" — as he shared his lesson topic — "then come to the left side of the room. If you want open practice, go to the right side of the room." It was such a simple approach, but it enabled both groups to feel welcome and get what they wanted in the space. Also, having more experienced dancers in the space provided mentorship opportunities for the newer dancers. Tafiya provided a space that embodied the "each one teach one" mentality of hip hop culture. He sensed an opportunity, responded to it, and created a high-impact solution that was even more inclusive.

We learned through our experiences. By putting the right people in the right roles, we trusted we could empower them to use their intuition. If something isn't going well or something is on fire, do something about it. Don't wait to ask if you can jump in, just do what you feel is right. We applied common sense and utilized the best strengths of our team. We needed the right people who could jump into the deep end and apply their intuition to challenges as they arose.

Each member of the Unity crew developed their expertise and honed their intuition while working in their respective field. It was this capacity for learning that was a big part of why we chose them to work at Unity. Cat was a hip hop dancer, focused on building our community programs; Marcel "Frost" DaCosta was a community-engaged b-boy who built our Mississauga hub program; Bob Veruela took Unity's national programs to the next level, pulling from his previous experience helping to build Graffiti Art Programming in his home town, Winnipeg. We let each of them shine in those roles while respectfully challenging them to always do better.

Mahad Shoaib was a youth who participated in Unity's after-school program in 2009. He was a natural leader when in the program, so we kept giving him more and more responsibility. Once he graduated high school and went to university, Mahad got involved as a volunteer in Unity. Almost a decade later, he applied for a full-time job and was hired from among many qualified candidates. It was another full-circle moment for truly involving participants' voices in the fabric of the organization; in Mahad's case, from dancing in his high school gymnasium to working full-time at Unity.

Mahad learned to write grants and implement program evaluations, even though it had very little to do with his area of study at university. He was one of the hardest workers on the team, putting in countless hours to learn about grant writing and program evaluation and to adapt to a challenging new role. Eventually he hit his stride in both areas and raised a *ton* of money while bringing all teams together to measure program impact. While he was actually one of the youngest members of the team, he became the glue that held all our teams together. He was instrumental in creating a bridge across the organization, between fundraising, programs, finance, and evaluation. He learned by doing and created his own in-house processes through listening, learning, and always striving to be better.

Flipping Mentorship: Celebrate Supporters

We led by example showing the team that it is okay to ask for help. We often brought in board members, topic-specific advisors, and knowledgeable volunteers to help the organization's creative side to become more operational. Whether it was a one-off review of a process for a second opinion or developing the finance committee (which helped us create a robust quarterly reporting and financial accountability structure), we always strived to be better.

Truly involving these often unlikely outside, professional perspectives helped engage a wider network of board members, mentors, advisors, and ultimately supporters of Unity. It helped us recruit the *right* board members and create a relationship where they were tasked with doing real, meaningful work. People loved coming to Unity events because they would engage with an unlikely group of amazing people from different backgrounds, bringing them together with a shared purpose.

We believed in celebrating success by acknowledging those who built key parts of Unity's foundation. In addition to our annual Celebrating Supporters event, on our ten-year anniversary, the team came up with the idea to honour key contributors to Unity's success by creating a Wall of Fame. We paid Rei Misiri, a visual artist on the Unity roster, to build and paint a creative display for the office that named everyone who contributed to Unity's continuous development. Rei painted names in silver calligraphy for those who gave two to four years of their energy to build Unity. We used gold letters for those who contributed five years or more. We also got silver- and gold-coloured pins for those whose names appeared on the wall. This included staff, artists, board members, and even volunteers — over 120 people in total. We wanted to create real pride in those who were part of this movement, because they deserved it.

TRUST: A DOUBLE-EDGED SWORD

Serious question: Do staff need to work in the same space? I think that building a connection between the people I work with is necessary, however, how often is it necessary for people to be face-to-face? I believe people are most productive when they have space to create and their time is respected. To have a workplace that supports their lives in and outside of work while getting shit done.

At Unity, it was about striking the right balance between self-care and productivity. I experimented with this idea a lot with the team. We needed to evolve our structures as we evolved as an organization. After about a decade, we landed on a higher-level strategic meeting format for managers; we called these "leadership meetings," and paired them with full staff meetings. This meeting structure prepared us to have deeper discussions on the ground level with the full team where everyone had an opportunity to be heard.

We held these meetings on Monday mornings, realizing that it was a great way to start the week, and rotated weekly between leadership meetings and full staff meetings. This allowed us to hold high-level strategic discussions with managers one week and then get into the details the next week with the full staff. Really, it took several years to figure out what meeting frequency, structure, and timing worked best, but when we landed on it, it resulted in improved accountability and clearer lines of communication.

This meeting structure evolved as the organization grew. When we had three employees, we only needed to hold staff meetings when necessary. We eventually got to half a dozen or so staff and got so busy that we held a staff meeting every month. Then we realized we needed to communicate as a team more often, so we tried out weekly staff meetings. Not surprisingly, we got annoyed that we were spending so much time in meetings, so we moved the meetings to bi-weekly. When we grew to fifteen staff, we needed to split the meetings up into different groups. We eventually started weekly one-on-one check-ins for managers to support their direct reports to achieve their short- and long-term goals. It was a constant and sometimes painful evolution of processes and structure as we responded to the increasing pressure points of our growth.

Meetings allow us the opportunity to assess what is getting done and what challenges are getting in the way of meeting goals. But outside of meetings, there has to be trust that work is moving ahead.

Fostering accountability was not my strong suit. I thought it was weird when staff told me they would do something and did not deliver. I was that kid in school who did my homework the day it was assigned, not the day it was due. This ensured that if I got sick or an emergency came up, I would never miss a deadline. I soon learned most people don't operate this way.

In 2017 we were submitting an application to a federal funder for a major government grant. This could result in a big chunk of money to support our national program expansion: $250,000. The grant was due on a Sunday evening, and our grant writer waited till the last minute to submit. What I didn't realize was that I needed to electronically sign the grant before we submitted, and I only found out I had to sign it a few hours before it was due. When I tried to log in to the portal, I couldn't remember my password and could not reset it because I'd forgotten the answers to my security questions. I panicked. We called the grant helpline, but because it was Sunday there were no answers. Tears began forming in my eyes, but I knew we needed to just keep trying. We wrote a long email explaining the situation to the grant officer handling the submissions. On Monday, as soon as their office opened, we called the grant officer to explain what happened. They were incredibly generous to let us still submit our application after the deadline. Months of work had gone into preparing this, and the experience taught our entire team that we needed to be more professional regarding submissions like this, and never leave things to the last minute. In the end, we received $225,000 from the funder. The stress of the experience was horrible, but sometimes the only way to learn is to nearly get burned.

As a leader at Unity, I needed to learn to build accountability within the team while still giving them space to dream. This was challenging, as I sometimes avoided having difficult conversations. I learned that in order to create more accountability, I had to make decisions, face conflict, and give immediate feedback. I learned the hard way that I leaned too much on trust and sometimes people took advantage of that.

Does trusting people always work? No. Trusting without boundaries presented some problems. There were times when staff showed up late or didn't complete their work on time or at all. They took advantage of my trust. For some, though, this deep trust created a climate for the level of independence and challenge they thrived on. I believe the right balance of accountability and trust is the key to building a thriving and high-performing culture. Trust was a bit of a double-edged sword at times though. Eventually we introduced frameworks and processes that held people accountable and could provide the checks and balances we needed. Some of these systems involved weekly check-ins with managers, annual performance reviews with goals and objectives, seasonal program evaluation, quarterly budget reviews, and semi-annual department reports. Empowerment and accountability were a constant balancing act as the organization evolved.

Flipping Management: Trust Works Both Ways

I learned something fundamental about trust at a staff retreat in 2014. I had a policy of being copied on *every* email from *every* employee. I didn't realize how much this was disempowering the team. I was doing it because I cared so much about the details, but I learned that this was caring expressed in the wrong way. At the end of the retreat, the team had an intervention with me. They told me that I needed to trust them and stop reading their emails. I listened and stopped being copied on everyone's email starting that night. It seemed so obvious, but it was an epiphany for me. The very thing I thought was helping was actually harming. I went from getting 250 emails per day to fifty. My team became more open to talking to me honestly — they began to trust me because they knew that I really trusted them, and took this trust with great responsibility. I was no longer looking over their shoulder. It was the difference between them having real and artificial authority.

From then on, we developed a new level of trust and communication with each other. I constantly reminded staff that I trusted them while continuing to challenge them in new areas. They did the same to me. Being someone who speaks too much, this was a constant challenge: I had to learn to listen. I reminded people at all levels to share their ideas and be honest, and I then did my best to create an open environment for feedback and improvement.

When I was a teenager, we used to throw big parties at our house. My dad always came downstairs and told us, "The one rule in our house is there are no rules." He gave us his full trust and as a result everyone treated the space with respect. In doing so, my father was telling us that with trust and respect came a whole lot of rules that were implied, even if they weren't spoken. This is the same type of trusting approach I brought to Unity: not always articulated, but implied that with this trust, and in the absence of many rules, came responsibility.

I had to evolve from being a micro-manager to becoming a more empowerment-focused leader. I encouraged staff to tell me the things they are the most uncomfortable to say about their work. How could we improve Unity? What could I do better to support their success? It allowed new space for working through difficult issues and making a better work environment for all. I can't support what I don't know, especially when I was the one causing a problem and no one felt comfortable telling me. This was very hard for me, as my natural inclination has always been avoid conflict, but I eventually learned to ask for more direct feedback.

Along with flexible and accommodating work schedules, we encouraged a dress code that allowed people to be themselves so we were never "selling" something we were not. This helped us attract partners and funders that aligned with our values. I wore silly animal t-shirts to every meeting, even very important ones, as that is a part of who I am. If someone does not accept us for who we are, then we aren't meant to work together. I encouraged our team to wear whatever made them feel comfortable too. This concept of fully being who you are was backed up by understanding, respecting, and embodying Unity's values.

We implemented an annual three-day staff off-site at a cabin in Blue Mountain to bring the team together. The goal was to gather honest insights from the team, check in, plan strategy, and build authentic connection. It was an opportunity for the team to connect, engage, and be heard. Living together, cooking for each other, and sharing the space built deeper relationships amongst the team. Unity's culture wasn't created overnight. It was ever evolving and took a ton of patience, honesty, love, and trust to build.

HUMAN RESOURCES ARE NOT "HUMAN"

I remember attending human resources classes and thinking it was a waste of time. Fast forward a decade, and I couldn't have been more wrong. I learned very quickly, when I needed to fire someone at Unity for the first time, why HR was so important. We had mistakenly hired someone in an administrative role and quickly discovered she was in way over her head. It was glaringly obvious we needed to do something, and it was only her first day on the job. So, together with my program director, Andel James, we made our apologies and asked her to leave.

I felt sick to my stomach all week. Although to me human resources didn't feel very human, it was vital knowing when to cut ties. This honestly is one of the reasons why Unity is still around. If a person is not a good fit for Unity, Unity is often not a good fit for the employee as well. Even though there is nothing more painful to me than firing someone, I knew that we couldn't keep people who weren't a fit. No one wins. I didn't sign up to do things related to being a boss, especially HR issues, and that soon became the most stressful and time-consuming part of my job.

I learned the importance of documentation. I didn't even know what a performance evaluation was when we started Unity. We had no policies and no clue that we would need them — remember, I started Unity at the age of fifteen! However, every time something we didn't have was needed, we created it almost overnight: HR policies, job descriptions, goals and objectives, performance reviews, contracts, incident reports, a code of conduct, onboarding processes, termination protocol, interview processes, bonus structure, compensation grids — the list goes on. We put these tools into practice our way, one brick at a time. The industry standard rarely fit Unity. We almost always found or created an alternative way, and it seemed to work. We created the Unity version of process, policy, and structure.

One of the preventative mechanisms we put in place was an HR policy. We had created an HR policy manual with a consultant paid for by a grant we got from the Ontario Arts Council in 2012, but we never used the manual because we simply did not have the time or capacity to implement it. Four years later, the organization had twelve full-time staff, and we realized we really needed HR policies. We pulled the old manual off the shelf, made minimal revisions, and began using it. We were lucky that we had done that legwork early on, creating the manual before we actually needed it.

This was the same for performance reviews. We only started doing performance reviews for staff in 2014, and I only had my first performance review in 2016. I had never had my performance reviewed before that, and it was actually a little scary. We did a 360 review as a part of the performance review process, and the feedback from the team showed that the very things I thought were my strengths were, from their perspective, my weaknesses: My team wanted me to make decisions — I wanted to involve their voice in the process. My team wanted me to deal with conflict — I wanted to give people space to grow. My team wanted me to take care of myself so they could better take care of themselves. This was a big wake-up call for me. So I listened and evolved.

Flipping Operations: Knowing When to Walk Away from a Fight

We faced constant urgent issues and fires at Unity, more than I could ever have imagined. It seemed like my full-time job became being a firefighter or a crisis management specialist. I learned that instead of freaking out when I saw smoke, I would just try, as calmly as possible, to address the issue as quickly and effectively as possible. Adding panic to an already panicked situation only made it worse. At times, managing these crises made me feel like giving up as they often triggered my anxiety.

In 2016, we had six artists staying at a rental house in Vancouver while doing three weeks of programs in that city. The person who owned the house complained that the artists were making too much noise, which I was told by our team wasn't true. I talked to the program director to ensure the artists in the house were being respectful to avoid future complaints. A few hours later, I got a call from our program staff that the police had been called. No matter what I was doing at the time, this problem was now my top priority. It was a big fire, and we had to put it out fast. This happened while I was at a leadership development conference for one week in the mountains in Banff, trying to disconnect.

After following up with the team, I believed that things were sorted out. But then I got another call and was informed that the police were called again and a report had been filed by the homeowner. My anxiety peaked. I tried to stay calm and think. I called the police and inquired about the situation. I soon found out that the homeowner was known for "causing issues," so the police told us not to worry about it. However, I was worried because we had just paid seven grand upfront for almost three weeks to rent this property and it was only the second day of the rental. To make matters worse, we had a report being filed with the police that could harm Unity's reputation. On top of all of this, we had a sponsor banner delivered to the house in Vancouver, which the homeowner signed for and refused to return it to our staff. UPS confirmed delivery of the banner and had the signature of the homeowner on record. Something wasn't adding up.

That same day a private investigator hired by the homeowner showed up to the house with an audio recorder to document the incident. Then, I received a phone call from a national body that rates charities in Canada. They told me someone had called them to report a complaint against us. This homeowner was now slandering our name publicly, and there was nothing we could do. I stepped out of my conference session in Banff and called my board chair, which resulted in a call to our lawyer. Our lawyer helped us draft a letter to send to the homeowner explaining what was happening from our perspective, instructing the homeowner to stop making false claims against us. We agreed to walk away and rent another space and take the loss. Not surprisingly, the homeowner emailed us two weeks later saying we flooded their washroom and she was not only keeping the full payment for the rental but also our damage deposit. It was a truly scary moment as we were caught in the middle of completely ridiculous and false claims against us, and our reputation was at stake. Instead of fighting fire with fire we walked away. We learned some battles are not worth fighting.

We created processes based on what we felt was right and then repeated them. Each year we created several new processes and policies to make Unity better and prevent future fires. We eventually also started tracking our risk management by creating a list of potential risks and how we were mitigating them at a board level. We put out fires, we prevented fires, and slowly we grew.

LETTING STAFF OWN SUCCESS AND FAILURE

We developed programs and departments in Unity from the ground up. We were constantly building the plane while flying it. I would do each job alongside each employee until we figured out their process, or until I got in their way. Eventually they gained my full trust, owned their departments, took responsibility for their outcomes, their successes, and their failures.

Over time, I began to allow more and more distance between me and the functional areas of Unity, eventually enabling staff to present their processes and program plans to me, showing me how they best work while co-creating clear goals and objectives. This gave staff the freedom to create their processes while our weekly check-ins would allow me to provide feedback and ideas and challenge them. I eventually let go and trusted staff to manage their own teams without my involvement or say.

Eventually I had so much trust for our employees, I let certain team members hire their own staff. I did not feel it necessary to attend the interviews. This was a huge step for me, as over the first twelve years of Unity I signed off on every new hire. I became confident that my employees knew the organization's values so deeply that I could let them direct the hiring process for their departments. This was not blind trust. This let them own the successes and failures of their own hires, and to take responsibility if the person underperformed. I also began to let people manage their own department budgets. It was tough to let these aspects go, but it was necessary. I was slowly becoming less and less needed as the founder, letting go of one element after another. Eventually it got to a point where I was less busy because the weight of the organization was distributed amongst the team. Trusting the team gave me space to start thinking about my future role.

TRUST REFLECTION QUESTIONS

Reflect on how you build culture, trust, empowerment, and accountability in your team:

1. How can you build trust in your team? How can you empower your team?
2. In what ways can you build accountability? (Examples: structurally, processes, policies, decision-making models, and evaluation.)
3. How can you achieve your ideal balance of team empowerment and accountability?
4. What are your criteria for an ideal team member? What people, skills, and talent might you be overlooking in your recruitment process?
5. What expertise are you developing internally as you build your plane? What knowledge is missing that needs to be developed and learned?
6. How are you building the skills and supporting the career path of each of your staff and volunteers?
7. Think back to a great moment you had at work. What made this feel great? How can you create great moments for others at work?
8. What are free or cheap and simple ideas you can use right away to build team culture? (Consider brainstorming ideas with your team.)

PART 4

GROW
Planting Seeds for the Future

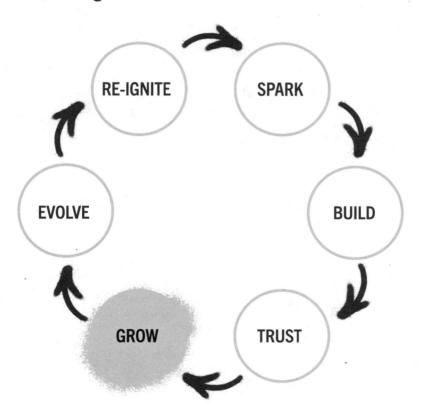

Hip hop is a visceral connection between the environment and the moment. It's a response in perfect harmony with music, the cypher and the people you're vibing with. It is energy you get from the crowd but also from inside. That burst of controlled yet spontaneous movement that leads to unimaginable one-of-a-kind flow in each moment. It's either perfectly executed or leaves you collapsed on the floor from not properly calculating the elements. You must make a decision in milliseconds. There is no right, no wrong, no perfect way. It's about character. Personality. You within the dance. Your alter ego. The untold story inside you. Elevating strength, improving weakness. Activating your superpowers. You choose your path. No one can tell you what to do. You are in the driver's seat. It is freedom of the body, mind, and inner desire. It allows us to use our body in ways we never could have dreamed. Challenging what it means to be human. Pushing limits of will and potential. This is breakin', my inspiration for creativity, growth, and testing new ideas in real time.

It would be delusional to think that Unity could have real impact alone. We understood that we were part of a much larger ecosystem that is interconnected and constantly changing. Knowing this made me constantly reflect, as we built Unity, on the space that our organization was taking up in the sector, community, and economy. This is important space — space that could be occupied by other organizations and other things. The non-profit sector has limited resources, and sometimes large-scale growth can take away from another organization in the funding ecosystem. The "pie" of resources in our sector is finite and is relied upon by all non-profits and social-purpose organizations; it is our duty to be responsible stewards of those funds. Understanding this propelled me to ensure that our programs represented the voices and needs of our community. It always made me think twice before trying to grow the organization.

This awareness of the ecosystem pushed me to reflect on several questions: What is the ideal size for Unity as an organization in terms of staff, funding, and resources in order to achieve the best impact for our mission? At what point does our quality or connection to community diminish as we grow? How can we prevent our impact from getting watered down as we grow? How do we maintain our values as we grow? What does responsible growth look like? I asked myself, "What is the right size for Unity?"

We don't ask enough questions about scaling responsibly in the non-profit sector — and in the world in general. Before Unity introduced a new program, for example, we spent a lot of time assessing the impact that program would have. We needed to have as much certainty as possible that we were moving in the right direction, before committing to growth. It is easy to get caught up in the idea that all growth is good for the organization and the community, but organizations

138   BUILDING UNITY

considering scaling need to have ways of measuring whether new initiatives or programs will have their desired impact. Or how large the need is that the organization can address. Or whether there are existing organizations that already offer these resources that could be partnered with to better serve their target community.

Growing responsibly is difficult because it requires a ton of internal and external reflection and collaboration, and the questioning of organizational assumptions. It takes time and investment to be responsible about growth. Sometimes organizations unintentionally reduce their effectiveness because they don't know how to manage growth. Organizations may even lose their values or connection to their community as they grow. It is important to remain focused on quality with growth and not get excited just because a growing reputation is having a positive effect on fundraising. Growth did not only happen in size at Unity, it also happened in scope, in quality, and in depth.

Early on at Unity, we scaled in size and learned a lot from this approach. As Unity's programs went into more and more communities, we had to look at their quality and degree of impact. We had to slow down a bit to focus on quality, from artist training to curriculum development to impact measurement. To have a deeper impact takes time, energy, community engagement, and resources. It was easy to get attracted to increasing numbers to satisfy funders, but we eventually realized we needed to go deeper, and that to do so, we had to slow down.

I remember our board chair Adam Silver telling us during a strategic planning session to reflect on the different types of scaling, not on just reach. Eventually we decided to write into our strategy to go deeper in our programming in year one, then, based on results and learning, to consider going wider in year two. As a team, we deemed it necessary to deep dive into quality before considering quantity. We asked ourselves:

How can program quality and connection to community be preserved as we grow?

What is the right type of growth for our organization?

How will we be able to sustain what we grow?

What negative impacts might we unintentionally have as we scale, and how can we mitigate any negative impact?

As we grow, who else in the community is not receiving this funding?

There are no easy answers to these questions, but I think they are questions and conversations leaders don't explore often enough when growing their idea in the wider ecosystem of non-profits and social-purpose organizations.

Flipping Sustainability: The "Pie of Support"

Organizations sometimes scale simply because it seems like the right thing to do. I didn't want Unity to be a product of tunnel vision, built from ego-busting ideas of how to change the world, because it had changed me. I wanted it to create respectful and sustained change on a tangible, human, person-to-person level. That is what we tried to focus on at Unity, creating a responsible impact. We were not just growing for growing's sake, although sometimes we were pulled in this direction and learned our lesson. We adopted and nurtured an "always-learning" approach to the impact we were having. This was our way of addressing the shortcomings of the "pie of support" that exists within the non-profit ecosystem.

The pie represents the limited number of resources available to community organizations, whether they be from government, corporations, individual donors, or revenue from social enterprise. I had this pie in mind as we grew. I attempted to help grow this pie of opportunity for others when possible, while taking the amount we needed to grow Unity. It was a careful balance. Sometimes we were in a situation where we felt like we were competing for the same slice of pie with peer organizations. It is very hard to let this feeling of competition go, but I don't look at the sector as competitive. If we are out to address social issues, we have to take the big picture into account. We must share our piece of the pie.

Another strategy is to try to bake new or bigger pies. This could be advocating funders and donors to give more because the need is increasing in a particular area. It could involve petitioning government, as a collective of organizations, to provide more money to causes from a similar category that are being overlooked. It could also involve pitching a case to philanthropists or corporations to consider giving away more money annually based on mutual goals. I advocated with a group of non-profits for the City of Toronto to invest nine hundred thousand dollars in new funding, over three years, to help stabilize six different arts-based organizations building emerging talent in our city for over a decade. It's even helpful to engage donors in the process of donating more so they understand the ecosystem approach instead of the competitive approach to funding. The more we buy into the competitive mentality, the more we lose sight of the big picture. There were times when we would decide not to apply for grants which raised funds in areas that were outside of our core programs, not only because it would stretch our capacity (through building new programs) but because we felt it was not right for us to be taking away from other charities in that space that were experts with limited resources.

Unity often lost out on revenue opportunities because some funders donated their entire budgets to one or two charities. Despite Unity's mandate fitting their philanthropic goals and priorities, we were unable to even apply to their fund because one cause was taking the entire pie. I'm not suggesting giving to large charities is a bad thing, but we need to consider how much space we take up in this field in order to make room for more, often smaller, high-impact non-profits to operate successfully together. We can't solve the biggest social challenges alone; we need a diversity of organizations to make the change the world needs right now. In a way similar to how Boost invited Unity into a large-scale partnership to create a trauma-informed dance therapy program, we need to challenge ourselves to consider strategic partnerships between non-profits, governments, corporations, and communities in order to help society achieve larger goals and to not work in isolation.

EXPANDING TO REMOTE COMMUNITIES: ACTING ON AN INVITATION

Sometimes when working with funders there were conflicting realities. Should we accept money from funders that may be having a negative environmental impact? When we first worked up in remote high schools as well as a few Indigenous communities in Western Canada, we debated this point at length amongst the team. At first, a few funders from the energy sector in the area advocated to bring us out and meet people in the communities to see if the high schools and local Indigenous communities might be interested in having us run programs. We flew out to several communities, met locals, and learned more about their needs for arts programs. After several conversations and in-person meetings, they asked us to come back and run programs. Schools and community leaders told us that youth were in need of engaging artistic outlets to help them cope with the many challenges they faced.

We engaged and involved the communities as we tested out different adaptations of our programs. We met with community leaders, schools, Elders, artists, and local non-profits to learn, partner, and collaborate. We involved artists and staff with experience working in remote Indigenous communities. These programs involved ongoing communication, local outreach, new training for our frontline artists, new artists with additional expertise on our roster, local community partnerships, and integrating the voices of the community.

Eventually several schools and communities found their own funding to invite us out to run programs throughout the year. We partnered with several local community organizations, schools, First Nations bands, and municipalities. We eventually secured local funding outside of the original companies that brought us out to shift our revenue streams to more sustainable sources to continue the programs. Our goal was to move away from funders who had potentially harmful impacts and we slowly made this shift while sustaining the programs over several years.

The community informed us that youth were in critical need of positive outlets to cope with the ongoing stress from recent forest fires that had had a detrimental impact on the community. We did our best and evolved our approach as we learned more. We could not just sit back and do nothing after the extensive conversations we'd had with communities, schools, youth, artists, and partners advocating for us to run programs. At the same time, we needed to be conscious of where our funding was coming from and always push to find revenue sources that were a better fit to sustain programs in the long run.

PLANT THE SEEDS, EVEN IF THEY DON'T GROW

At Unity, the less we followed what other non-profit and business leaders did, and the more we did what we felt was right, the more we succeeded and stood out. This especially pertained to fund development — a.k.a. "the hustle" — which is key to any business or non-profit for longevity. We were always hustling: running great programs, selling authentically, and maintaining good relationships.

The hustle is hard work in the right places, and those right places for me were programming and fundraising. I realized that fundraising had to be constant and strategic or we wouldn't survive. We could never take a break from revenue generation. As soon as we got one large grant or donation, I would already be pitching to the next five potential donors, planning pitches for the next ten, and researching the next thirty.

If we needed five thousand dollars, we would apply for twenty-five thousand. In the beginning, we were in a market where no one knew our name or understood what we were doing, so this approach was the only way for us to stay alive. I mean, honestly, who had ever heard of a hip hop charity with the goal of improving youth mental health? We needed to hustle hard to get in the door, and at first it was an uphill battle.

In 2005, when I was 19 years old, our first corporate funder, Freedom 55 Financial, gave us five thousand dollars for winning first prize at the Courage to Soar pitch competition as part of a conference put on by the Top 20 Under 20 program. I pitched against an eight-year-old, who raised millions of dollars for tsunami relief, as well as other incredible young people. I pitched the Hip Hop Away from Violence program to expand to five new schools in underserved communities. Somehow my project won the pitch. The judges told me I made a clearer case for support than the others who pitched, by providing a defined need, budget, and plan.

After the competition was finished, I met with Murray Parks from Freedom 55 Financial and made a pitch for their continued support. The company trusted in us and slowly grew its support over ten years to become a national partner with support coming from their national parent company, Great West Life. Every year I would grab lunch with the two staffers who were ongoing internal champions for Unity. Eventually one of them, Jodi Weber, joined our board of directors and fundraising committee. She remains an active contributor to Unity, and personal mentor to me. We were able to lock in multiple three-year national partnerships with Great West Life. This was one of many long-term funding relationships we built and maintained.

We were always looking at ways to diversify our funding model and create multiple streams of revenue, so we were not reliant on any one funder. In my observations with other charities, having to depend on one big donor can have detrimental consequences if the donor reduces or cuts its funding suddenly. In today's environment, these cuts happen often, and charities are closing down even after decades of being in operation. Some organizations depended on the provincial government for 80 percent or more of their funding. When the province cut its direct funding to organizations, many had no other option but to close their doors. Diversifying revenue was a survival tactic for Unity.

That isn't to say that Unity never experienced funding cuts. Usually, two to six major funders would drop out every year, and we would lose between $25,000 and $100,000 per funder. There was natural attrition as funders changed their priorities.

By 2017 Unity had an annual operating budget of $1.4 million. We had successfully diversified our revenue across multiple sources. The revenue streams looked like this:

corporate funders: 40%
government: 29%
individual donors: 10%
private foundations: 8%
social enterprise: 13%

Our largest funder that year accounted for 19 percent of our overall budget. Our biggest job was to maintain, upsell, and juggle our top fifty funders who gave between five thousand and a hundred thousand dollars. With this strategy, Unity could remain relatively secure as funders changed their priorities, and we also had growing revenue streams from corporate events and fees from school shows paid by school boards and principals. At the same time, we were constantly prospecting and researching new potential sources of revenue. We never wanted to have an entire program — or even worse, the entire organization — be overly dependent on any one funder. We started small with many funders and that allowed us to be nimbler. Eventually that led us to growing some of the better-aligned funders over time, and this gave us flexibility in our model and ability to respond to urgent need in the community.

We got ourselves in the door in whatever way we could, worked really hard to positively impact the lives of the young people we worked with, and had consistent and open communications with our funders. We over-communicated, which funders often did not expect, and we focused on building relationships. Funders told us we went above and beyond in engaging them with our cause, in comparison to other charities they supported. One funder once told me, "You punch way above your weight." In addition to filling out the standard funding reports, we always asked our donors how we could be a better partner and provide more opportunities for engagement. We invited them to see our programs, brought lunch-and-learn workshops to their offices, performed at their corporate conferences and parties, customized creative activations in line with their business goals, presented them with awards at our annual Celebrating Supporters events, invited their family to be VIPs at our festival, and much more. Because of our approach, we were able to often transition these into multi-year partnerships by exceeding their expectations and then increasing our ask.

We didn't want to over-ask and scare away funders, but we equally didn't want to ever have to shut down programs or let staff go due to lack of funds. It was always a balancing act to build a healthy reserve while maintaining reasonable expectations for all stakeholders. We always had three to six months' worth of operating funds in the bank during my entire time at Unity. We built resilience into the fabric of our organization through a diversified fundraising strategy. We were like a cactus in the desert: We built a reserve of funding as a cactus builds a reserve of water to survive in harsh conditions. As we grew the organization, we grew our cactus spikes to be long and sharp, ensuring the protection of the organization from the environment. We did our best to prepare for dry periods. We were building resilience to create a more sustainable organization.

What we learned as we built Unity was that there was natural turnover with funders, even if the relationships were good. So the challenge was to be constantly adding new supporters at a faster rate than donors would drop off. How could we continue to retain existing donors while at the same time finding new donors? This to me is the fundraising challenge. Survival of the fittest. Creating redundancies so we were never too dependent on one big funder. We became professional jugglers. It's an intense yet worthwhile hustle. Instead of having four funders giving $250,000, have a hundred $10,000 funders. After over a decade, we had secured fifty major funders and two hundred individual donors annually. This is what allowed us to grow steadily and never have to fire someone or close a program because of a loss in funding. It is because we hustled to diversify our revenue sources. Can I sustain what I've already created? Can I also grow that at the same time? Our revenue pipeline is what kept us going, and if we lost a big funder, I lost some sleep until we found a few new ones or grew an existing one. Unity was able to grow consistently because revenue grew as the organization did. Strongly diversified fundraising kept our mission alive.

UNITY'S REVENUE PIPELINE: WE GREW WITH CREATIVITY AND PERSEVERANCE

Our revenue pipeline was a living document. It was an excel file we used to track all of our funders from confirmed in the bank to those being researched as potential funders.

Through our revenue pipeline we would research hundreds of potential funders, pitch twenty most likely funders to support, submit ten proposals for pitches that went well, and aim to get funding from half or more applications. It was simply about learning to qualify donors that we thought were likely to support Unity and putting them through this revenue pipeline process. Eventually we were able to roughly predict how much we might receive based on results from previous years. This helped us create diverse revenue streams and sustain organizational stability.

In a few basic steps, here is how we made sure that the revenue pipeline was a living, breathing document that ensured everyone in the organization was aware of where funding was coming from and where our next funding targets lay:

- Kept an up-to-date prospect list of potential funders with contact information, deadlines, guidelines, and follow-up history;
- Pitched as many warm leads as possible that were the best fit face-to-face;
- Submitted proposals where there was a fit;
- Followed up relentlessly until we heard back;

- Confirmed funding, ran programs, reported back results;
- Engaged donors and their families so they would grow their support in future.

For example, we were able to fund our after-school program with an overall budget of around $200,000: $50,000 from a corporate funder; $50,000 from a private foundation; $30,000 from fees from school boards; $25,000 from another corporate funder; and $45,000 from another private foundation. We had to juggle these relationships to help sustain the program, but if we lost one of these funders at any point, we could go to the others to ask for additional support. We would either try to upsell an existing funder or bring in a new funder that we had been courting to fill the gap. We were constantly pitching new funders to simply get in the door at any amount. We would start with warm leads. We were always trying to get meetings with new potential funders from a warm contact, and we were most successful with warm intros championed from a current Unity supporter.

For referrals we targeted board members, current funders, people we met at corporate performances, and our fundraising committee. Worst-case scenario, we would just cold call someone on our list, and on occasion this strategy would work too.

We had a major private family foundation on our list for nearly seven years and could not get a warm introduction. We noticed this funder was one of the biggest funders for five other organizations that focused on arts education in the city. This foundation made significant contributions to these other organizations and offered multi-year support. We did our research. They were the perfect prospect for Unity, but we couldn't get an introduction from anyone we knew.

Eventually we got access to a funder database, and this foundation was on the list. We sent an email to a generic address for the foundation and unbelievably got a response in forty-eight hours to set up a meeting. I couldn't believe it. We pitched them at the meeting and very soon received confirmation of three years of support at sixty-five thousand dollars per year! Cold calls didn't work often for us, but in this case, we had no other option and it proved to be very successful. It showed us we needed to be open to trying different approaches when going after funding.

Once we got our foot in the door with a small donation, we would slowly pry the door open by building strong and engaged relationships. If funders said no to us, we would keep them on our list. Some funders remained on our prospect list for eight years before donating anything. Being persistent and respectful in our requests was key to breaking through. We would never give up on a prospect that was a good fit. We would ask for just a small donation to let us prove ourselves. If we received even a modest donation, we would engage the donor at five or ten times the value they were expecting. We would give a five thousand dollar first-time funder the engagement we would give a fifty thousand dollar funder. We had a list of creative options to engage our funders that we used to grow our relationships. From beatbox performances at staff holiday parties, to lunch-and-learn spoken word workshops to build team culture, to employees doing tags with our graffiti artists, we did anything we could to engage funders in unique ways. We wanted new donors to remember Unity. We needed to stand out. We leaned on our strengths, and by engaging funders and their teams so deeply, we created a strong case to increase our ask.

Flipping Sustainability: Align Partnerships to Mutual Goals

Unity's approach to thinking about fundraising was framed by the following questions, related to many of the aspects of building and maintaining our organization:

- Can we get a multi-year partnership?
- Can we get existing donors to increase their support?
- What new funders would be interested in this program that we can start courting, just in case we lose a key funder?
- What communities that we are working in are of interest to funders on our prospect list?
- How do we keep funders engaged so they stick around for five to ten years, instead of turning over every year?
- What foreign companies have just opened for business in Canada that have not chosen their charities for their corporate social responsibility strategy?
- What are the top hundred most profitable companies in Canada, and do they give to our cause?
- Which funders are giving to other charities similar to Unity?

Many of these questions relate to the fact that funders have different giving strategies. Some corporations want to have charitable programs they support running in places where they do business. A bank in a small town would support a local program to show its connection to the community. Other funders might be interested in an issue like the arts or poverty reduction, and so we would have to explore how we could connect Unity's mission to their priorities without stretching our mission.

It was important for Unity to deeply understand what fuels individual motivations for giving and if we could align with those priorities. There were some funders for whom we were a perfect fit, and for others we had to stretch to meet their needs. Many funders we would decide not to engage with because of lack of alignment. We made it a point to learn about their priorities, read their funding guidelines, and meet them face-to-face. We used to ask a long list of questions of funders to better understand their giving strategies and ensure the best fit and most strategic approach possible, including:

- How do you define your funding priorities? What are your main priorities?
- Who are some of your favourite groups you fund? What do they do that makes them great to work with?
- What is the average amount you fund for a project? What is the largest gift you currently give? What is a reasonable first ask?
- How can we best grow our funding relationship over time?
- Do you make multi-year commitments?
- Is there a difference between local and national asks?
- What budgets do your donations generally come from? Marketing? Community Investment? Corporate Social Responsibility? All of the above?
- Are there creative ways we can link our ask across multiple budgets within your company to enhance our opportunity for financial support?
- How does your giving tie to your business objectives?
- What results do you need to show to increase funding over time?
- Are there internal changes that you know about that may affect future funding or timing? (For

example, resources are being allocated to the launch of a new strategy, and you'll need to refocus priorities based on shifting budgets.)

- How do you want to be recognized for your support? May we use your logo on our website, marketing materials, and social media?
- Do you have any internal events we can get involved with? (Here we would pitch our ability to give inspiring keynotes, where we share our stories of impact, bring in high-energy performers, teach senior VPs breakin' routines to perform at major staff rallies, sell Unity gear, create interactive graffiti pieces, promote volunteer opportunities to employees, and brainstorm ideas with the prospective funder that would work best for their goals.)
- How can we integrate your staff in the partnership in creative and fun ways?
- Do you have any senior staff looking to join a board?

ACTING ON OPPORTUNITY: AN INVITATION FROM SAN PATRIGNANO

Subject: invitation to Italy — WeFree Days
Date: September 1, 2010

Dear Michael,

I'm very pleased to introduce you to San Patrignano, a therapeutic community based on Italy's Adriatic coast (sanpatrignano.org) and currently the world's largest residential drug treatment facility with 1500 residents. Professional training and social reintegration are two of the cornerstones of our rehabilitation program, and I think that your organization also infuses socially marginalized youngsters with a passion for the activity of dance and music, giving them the tools to express themselves, build self-esteem and learn valuable life skills.

Drug use among young people in Italy is reaching concerning levels, and for this reason young people from San Patrignano who have completed the program wish to tell their story, travel across the country bringing a prevention show to Italian students, in the hopes of connecting with them and creating a dialogue which can follow on the relative websitewefree.it (in the Italian language).

The reason I am writing to you now is that we are planning an event on next October 9th called "WeFree Days" to be held on the grounds of the community. Thousands of students from middle and secondary schools will participate, as well as representatives of Italian government, international bodies (such as the United Nations), volunteer associations, and those working in the field of social work and on related issues. The event will be divided into various thematic areas. In one called "Experience," more than 2000 students from all over Italy will be able to interact with representatives from "best practices" in the social field coming from across the globe. In another one, we will be organizing a roundtable discussion on socially related themes with speakers from the private and public sector.

Lastly, there will be an area called "theatre," where we will present the theatrical pieces that we have brought all over Italy as part of our prevention campaign over the past year. So I'm writing you to ask you if your organization would be interested in participating at this 2010 event to show to the thousands of young people, associations, representatives of national and international institutions who will attend the event, its work. We would like to see hands-on performances and, when possible, interactive demonstrations of how "Unity Charity" gets people passionate and involved in your programs.

We hope that you could be interested in this participation, and I invite you to watch a short video clip about last year's "WeFree Days" so that you can get an idea about what happened during 2009 editionwefree. it. Further information (in English) about the event will be available soon.

I apologize for not having been able to contact you earlier, but I hope to hear from you soon so that we can better discuss details of your participation. In the meanwhile I thank you very much for your attention and send you my best regards.

— Francesca

I received Francesca Ronchin's email on September 1, 2010. I noticed in the email that she had listed a Toronto telephone number. I was skeptical, but I wanted to act fast as Francesca said she had emailed a few Canadian organizations and only one would be chosen from each country using hip hop to engage youth. WeFree Days were only one month away. And so I called her.

She told me she was working for a self-sustained, high-impact social enterprise where over 1,500 people live to overcome alcohol and drug addiction. The organization didn't use doctors or drugs. It focused on reintegration through peer mentorship, workplace training, and harm reduction. Sounds questionable, right? I thought so too. On top of all of this, Francesca told me they wanted to bring Unity to work with teen-agers in Italy to help engage them in a conversation of drug prevention through hip hop performances and storytelling. Have you ever received one of those emails that asks you to wire money to a foreign country for a great opportunity that somehow made it past your spam filter? I was skeptical, yet open and intrigued to learn more, even if it seemed a little too good to be true.

I questioned her about everything she had told me in the email and soon realized this might actually be a real opportunity. She seemed impressed at how fast I got back to her. Francesca happened to be in Toronto, so we arranged to meet at a coffee shop in the Yonge and Eglinton area. I wanted to meet in a public space, just in case.

After the meeting — which went very well and answered any ques-tions I may have had about their credibility — I sent her our bios and more info on why Unity would be a great fit. Within one week she booked five flights to Italy for the Unity team. In October, three of Unity's top artists, Scott Jackson, Taeyeon "TK" Kim, and Jim "Nastic" Cartasano; Kareen Wong, a youth alumni from Uniteam; and I attended. Unity represented Canada amongst organizations from twelve countries offering hip hop programs. We met groups from Afghanistan, Uganda, Portugal, Cambodia, Columbia, Brazil, and many more, all using hip hop as a tool for positive social change. We immediately became part of a global community. All of a sudden I didn't feel so alone in the work we were doing.

San Patrignano is the most incredible social enterprise I have ever seen. The community is situated on hundreds of acres of natural beauty.

Each person who is recovering from an addiction is assigned a job and a peer mentor who has been through the program in the past, and they may live for several years in the community. Everything they need is there. They cook their own food, sew their own clothes, raise their own animals, pick the grapes for their own wine (yes, wine), and make their own furniture. Everything they make they sell for profit. It's a completely self-sustained social enterprise.

We ate all of our meals in the giant mess hall with the entire community. It felt magical. The meals were prepared by the community, and the food was delicious. I was shocked that they served alcohol, but their philosophy is that harm reduction is about being able to have things in moderation, so when people leave the community, they can enjoy wine with meals.

San Patrignano is one of the most innovative places in the world to break the cycle of addiction. For many it is a last resort, but San Patrignano has an incredible track record. It was a life-changing experience that I will never forget. It showed me the possibility of holistic impact and sustainable change around addiction.

We also ended up winning a performance competition WeFree held amongst the hip hop outreach groups who were there. The goal was to see who could create the most inspiring performance around WeFree's message of harm reduction and recovery from addictions for thousands of high school students.

We continued to go back to WeFree Days for five years following this initial connection. We gained a global perspective and network of hip hop outreach programs. We connected with outstanding groups like Breakdance Project Uganda (bouncingcats.com), who worked across Uganda teaching breakin' to youth with a particular focus on those who are disadvantaged to give them hope and opportunities. The project is centered on the belief that everyone can learn, and everyone can teach and has the capacity to be a positive role model to others. Another incredible group we got to exchange with was Tiny Toones from Cambodia (tinytoones.org), who teach breakin' and the arts as an incentive for kids living on the streets to get an education to aim for better employment outcomes.

WeFree had an incredible impact on anyone from our team who had the opportunity to experience this community, broadening our outlook on what is possible in terms of using hip hop as a tool to create social change. The international hip hop outreach community continued to grow and so did our belief in its potential. All from picking up the phone, being first to respond, and taking a chance on an opportunity.

I BECAME A PROFESSIONAL FIREFIGHTER

At Unity I learned to be open to any ridiculous thing that came our way. I became something of a professional firefighter. It seemed there was always a fire to put out, and every time I thought I'd seen it all, there was always something more unpredictable that came up.

In 2015 I received an email from someone who said he went to high school with me. I couldn't remember him, but there are a lot of people you only vaguely remember from high school. He told me he wanted to raise money for Unity through a raffle. Every time we receive an offer from someone we don't know to fundraise on behalf of Unity, we have to assess whether the individual has the skillset to do so. Our reputation is too important and major damage can be caused by having Unity associated with a fundraising activity not handled well. I tried to arrange a phone call with him to learn more about him and the raffle, but could never get him on the phone. Eventually I sent him a message to not run the fundraiser because we were never able to connect. After a while I forgot about it, and I assumed he had dropped the idea.

Two months later I got an email via Unity's website asking if we were running a raffle in a rural town north of the city. Red flag.

I knew something was fishy about that earlier interaction. I immediately responded and asked this person to call me. In our call, I learned someone had contacted them on Facebook, asking if they wanted to sell raffle tickets in this town for a split of the ticket sales. Fortunately they thought it was very suspicious and decided to get in touch with us directly. I asked them to scan all of the tickets and info they had been sent. I looked deeper into things and saw that the raffle tickets had a registered lottery number. This is required by law in the province of Ontario. In order to get this number, you require written approval of the charity being supported.

I started to get pretty nervous at this point. Did this guy forge documents to get a lottery licence in Ontario with our name on it? I called the Lottery and Gaming Commission to look up the number to see if it was forged. They looked into it and told me it was bogus and to call the police. Shit. Now there were fake raffle tickets out in rural communities across the province with our name on them, and some scam artist was making money off our name. I filed a police report, and we put a notice on our website that someone was running an illegal raffle with our name on it. There were some fires that happened at Unity that I never could have even dreamed up as possible. This was definitely one of them.

As Unity continued to grow, fires came up more often. We were a bigger target, which posed bigger risks. We needed to build processes to identify and reduce risk. We created a third-party fundraising policy to mitigate situations like this one (see the "Tools & Resources" section at end of this the book for a sample of this policy or visit epicleadership.ca/bookresources). We also created a risk management document for the board to identify all potential risks we could think of and what we could put in place to reduce the chances of those things from happening. We needed to plan ahead and prevent fires where possible. As we grew, the risk of failure grew. We needed to be ready for anything that came our way.

INNOVATING IN THE MOMENT: LET GRAVITY PROVE ME WRONG

If you watch an experienced b-boy or b-girl, you would think they get hurt a lot. Thankfully, the biggest injury I've ever had was a sprained pinky finger. The reason for lack of injury is that the risks I take are calculated, based on my previous experiences, and I can respond to what is happening in the moment. I learn to be attuned to responding in the present moment. If my right shoulder is hurting, I don't do power moves or freezes on that arm. I would focus more on toprocks (dance steps done standing up), and footwork (controlled variations of steps on all fours), or even choose not to dance at all until I healed. This is informed risk taking. It involves listening to my body and responding accordingly. The people I know who get injured often usually take risks and are not truly listening to their body. For me, this is much the same as creating an organization, taking calculated risks while building from strengths and working through pain points that are holding the organization back.

In breakin', if I dream up a move I try it. It's a space where I can make my dreams a reality. I believe now that anything is possible, which has led me to doing things I once thought impossible. Sometimes I'll have an idea that will take more than a decade until I'm able to execute it. I start with a dream, a big goal. I keep an abundant mindset, holding the belief that anything might be possible. This has created new possibilities for the dance and how it has evolved. It has also stretched my belief of what I am capable of. I keep pushing these boundaries, finding new angles, new moves, and new possibilities. We aren't going to solve complex challenges in the world by repeating failed attempts; we need to try innovative new ideas. I explore every corner I can think of to discover ideas I could only dream of; I believe anything can be done and let only gravity prove me wrong.

A big part of bringing new dreams to reality has been believing in the people around me to take ideas and run with them. Someone who constantly made new things possible at Unity was Rajni Sharma.

Rajni: Scaling Impact with Ambition and Humility

I consider Rajni one of Unity's best hires, although she was not obviously aligned on paper. She had a corporate job at a paper shredding company, but I knew after meeting her she was going to kill it with us. If we hadn't taken the chance to meet twenty people over two days when we were hiring for our festival coordinator, we would never have even met Rajni. When I met her, though, I could feel her passion and sincerity for the cause, and I sensed the strength of her character. She is the real deal. Something interested me about her corporate experience mixed with her involvement with a world music festival. After the interviews, she was one of two potential candidates for the position.

I always bring another staff member or two into interviews in order to help make a collective decision. We all agreed that Rajni was the best fit. She started as festival coordinator in 2012. In her first year, she cold called a local bank and got a sponsorship. We built that from a five thousand to a hundred thousand dollar annual partnership over seven years.

That same year, Rajni secured our first major international headliner to perform at Unity's festival, Talib Kweli. She also hired FLIP Publicity, a PR company, and we worked with Damien Nelson from their team to help get media coverage for us. FLIP Publicity promoted many of the major local festivals in Toronto. Rajni had never run a festival before. She just knew how to get shit done. I challenged her to go big and own it. She blew it out of the water.

After three years of running the biggest festivals at Unity, Rajni told me she wanted a change. She was just repeating the same thing she had done, but with a different list of artists and sponsors.

We sat down one summer day, and I asked her where she wanted to take her career and what she wanted to learn. Her big dream was to one day become an art therapist, which she was in school for while working at Unity. She also told me she could probably do more in fundraising. Trusting in her experience with the bank pitch and a few other festival sponsors, we gave it a shot. We posted her job as festival coordinator, she helped hire the new person to replace her, and then Unity promoted her into a new role as director of development and communications. For context, this title is usually given to people with fancy certifications and years of experience and education in fundraising. Rajni had never done fundraising before, but I knew she could figure it out. She'd somehow figured out how to run a festival that attracted over thirty thousand attendees! If she set her mind to something, Rajni would turn big ideas into reality.

So, we began again.

How do we run a major festival? Let's figure it out.

How do we raise a million dollars? Let's figure it out.

New challenges excited us both. We eventually came up with a formula where we would get a warm introduction to a potential corporate funder, pitch them face-to-face, follow up with a proposal, and follow up until she got a confirmation. Rajni helped Unity raise over five million dollars, building the organization to levels I never would have dreamed. As we grew, she became my trusted strategic critic and first line of support when things were on fire. She held the plane together. She was an amazing leader and truly empowered those who reported to her on the team. She challenged staff, artists, and alumni to own their impact while caring deeply about their well-being. She was so humble about her contribution that very few people really knew how much she really did.

At Unity we were building our track record or, as we do in hip hop, "showing and proving." At the same time, the program had to have positive and ideally measurable impact or there was really no point in doing any of this work to begin with. Unity's evaluation committee designed pre and post surveys to evaluate program impact and gather data for internal and external stakeholders. We used validated surveys to measure impact on youth mental health and resilience. These survey tools had prior research behind them to test if the questions would provide reliable results when asked in populations similar to those we served at Unity. We added our own questions to the surveys to gather additional data specific to the quality of our programs.

We hired an evaluation consultant to help us select a validated survey tool that youth would not find intimidating. The consultant we brought on, Matthew Hughsam, researched a long list of validated survey tools and asked youth in our programs for their feedback. Eventually we landed on a survey that youth felt comfortable completing and which produced quality results. Matt helped us build a community engagement approach to evaluation. University students ran focus groups as a class project to match qualitative testimonials with quantitative survey data. This comparison helped us determine if there was consistency across the different sets of data we were gathering. Evaluation results helped us identify patterns of what was working and where we could improve. We slowly built our reputation by running programs, gathering data, learning and sharing the story. We also used evaluation data to improve programs, identify needs for staff and artist training, and revise program curriculum and processes. Evaluations helped us share the story and understand our impact, which helped keep our funders, stakeholders, and community engaged and informed. Run programs, gather results, learn, improve, grow, repeat.

WE HAVE LIFTOFF! SEED FUNDING THAT LAUNCHED UNITY

Our very first grant proposal, in 2008, was to the Laidlaw Foundation. Laidlaw staff were amazing. They generously coached us, reviewed our application, and helped along the way as mentors. The title of grant *officer* doesn't reflect the folks at Laidlaw; they were really grant *partners*. Laidlaw treated us like an equal in this relationship, which was a breath of fresh air. After six months of waiting, we got the news. We received our first grant for $38,023 from Laidlaw. I couldn't believe it. I remember crying on the phone when Ana Skinner, the grant officer at Laidlaw, told me. I was overwhelmed. Our dream was becoming real. We were no longer volunteers.

I immediately knew what we needed to do next. We went into program development and fundraising hyperdrive. We hired three people: Julla, Malik, and me. Everyone was part-time, at minimum wage, including me. We needed to find a way to pay people properly so we could retain staff. It seemed like our goal was impossible. What we needed to figure out was how to pay competitive wages, but we were so dependent on grants. We were running on passion and minimum wage for much longer than we would have liked to, but we soldiered on until funders began to trust in our slowly building reputation.

In 2009 we targeted three major funds: Ontario Trillium Foundation, Ontario Arts Council, and the Toronto Arts Council. Malik and I built a pitch that told the full story, our track record, and why they could trust us, even though I was just a teenager wearing silly t-shirts, a sideways baseball cap, and sweatpants. We set up meetings with all three grant officers and pitched our story.

Everyone seemed intrigued yet hesitant, but we still needed to get through the grant-writing and peer-review decision-making process. My first mission was to get some multi-year funding because year-to-year project funding was not sustainable. All three funders advised us not to go for multi-year funding. I repositioned the question. Instead of asking whether Unity would be considered for multi-year funding, the new question was, "Would you even look at our application if we submitted for multi-year or operating funding?" Surprisingly, this new question produced different answers. Two said they would look at it but most likely wouldn't fund it, and one said not to bother. This was amazing news: two funds would consider an application for multi-year funding! It was in this moment that we learned we needed to ask specific questions when meeting potential funders to gather data on the best strategic approach.

Once we got permission, we went for it. Even though the "you can do that" had quickly been followed by "but I don't think it will be successful," it was still enough for me. There was a chance. It took about two months for Malik to write all three applications. We applied for a single-year project fund for the one grant that would not accept an application for multi-year funding. Then the wait began, and four months later we got three responses. The most straightforward one was the Toronto Arts Council, the project grant. We got it! Woo-hoo! The second one was from the Ontario Trillium Foundation. The way that grant works is you can apply to different regions at one time (or as they called them "catchments"), and each catchment has a different board of volunteers that decides which applicant will receive funding. We applied for three regions: Toronto, Peel, and York. They called, letting me know we got denied by Toronto and York region, but they had some good news. If we cut our budget by one third, Peel was interested. I hesitated for a moment, calculating the numbers in my head, and said, "Let's do it!"

This was the benefit of applying for multiple grants at one time: it gave us some wiggle room within program budgets if we didn't receive full funding, which is exactly what happened. At one of the organizations, we applied for operating funding, which is generally unheard of for new organizations. It is really difficult to get operating funding as a first-time applicant because funders usually ask you to first apply for project grants as a testing ground for your organization. There was also a long line of organizations that compete for operating funding, and we didn't have much of a track record yet. We applied for operating funding even though the organization said its operating funds were already fully spent and it had no additional budget room.

Then I got a call from this funder. Operating funding had come through. Unbelievable. Our timing had been perfect, as one organization had been defunded in that round of decisions, giving space for one new, emerging group to receive an operating grant. Good thing we put ourselves out there at that time. The grant officer advocated for Unity because she believed in our work, as did the decision committee that reviewed our grant proposal. All combined, we had our first $10,000 from Toronto Arts Council, $65,000 from Trillium, and $20,000 from Ontario Arts Council, plus $20,000 from the Toronto Foundation. We surpassed $100,000, money that went directly into programming and driving the next phase of growth. This gave us a solid year to run some great programs and fundraise as fast and as hard as possible.

In the third year we wrote seventeen funding applications and received grants from ten, raising just over two hundred thousand dollars. We had made it to the next pressure point of growth and were building momentum. It was time to evolve once again.

I realized that being genuine and honest built lasting connections with donors. My dad always taught me to be honest when growing up. He always led by example (even if it got him into trouble); his actions spoke louder than words. That's why Unity did not spend huge amounts of money to raise money. It didn't feel genuine or necessary to waste money to impress people to donate. We stood out because we did things we thought made sense and leaned into our strengths.

I think it's silly to spend large amounts of money on events that raise money. It just didn't feel right or sincere. My theory was if people truly care about the cause they will give. I knew we could run a top quality, high-impact event without spending a ton of money. No one wants to go to a fundraiser where the money isn't going to the cause, yet so many galas have huge overhead costs. If I am donating to a charity, I want the money to go to the cause, not some fancy dinner. For some reason so many organizations still run these incredibly wasteful events. It baffles my mind.

At our VIP fundraiser in 2018, we raised over two hundred thousand dollars, and 96 percent of the funds went directly to the cause. This event cost eight grand in total. Over five years of hosting this fundraiser, we raised more than half a million dollars and spent less than 8 percent of the funds raised on event costs. In the end there was very little waste, and we accomplished the same goal: by being resourceful, we raised a bunch of money that went directly to benefitting the youth in our programs. We also communicated to our donors very clearly that we don't waste their money. If something didn't make sense to us, we followed our gut and did things our way.

We did what we felt was right, but we weren't afraid to engage our funders and donors in conversations to help us figure out how to do things differently. We asked for advice. We would meet our big funders as often as possible to brainstorm ideas on how we could further engage the partnership. The funny thing is, they would often tell us how to get more money from them if we asked. We seemed to be rising above well-known charities in a very competitive environment for funding. Every few years I heard of long-standing charities closing down due to lack of funding, and yet here we were growing rapidly. We stood out, and Unity thrived.

We performed for corporate staff engagement events across the country, became part of co-branded national ad campaigns and even got the CEOs of several of Canada's largest corporations dancing with us in front of thousands of their employees!

In 2012, when Rajni contacted the local bank to ask for a small sponsorship for the Unity festival, the first pitch meeting really reinforced for me the need to be myself and hopefully attract the sort of people that fit Unity's mission. In the meeting, I joked about dropping my pants during my pitch — "Hip hop is not about people with their pants to their knees trying to act cool," I said as I pulled my pants below my waist and proclaimed, "Oh shoot, I just pulled my pants down in a really important business meeting" — and everyone burst out laughing.

The next year we grew the partnership to fifty thousand dollars. We built the relationship through deeper engagement with the bank's staff. We met monthly to discuss ways to strengthen the partnership. The relationship flourished. Two years later we asked them to increase their support and received over a hundred thousand dollars annually. Once at this level, the bank flew a small team of Unity artists, including myself, across Canada to perform at their staff engagement events. We also ran workshops for youth in each city on this cross-Canada tour. The bank became our most engaged partner.

The bank's president, Peter Aceto, became genuinely interested in what we did, and so I asked him if he would be interested in joining our board. After getting to know Peter through the events I was surprised that someone in such a senior role was so down to earth, generous, and genuine. I knew this was a long shot but thought I would ask. At first, he seemed unsure if he could commit, but he told me he was very interested. After a few weeks of following up, I pretty much gave up. Why would the president of a bank want to join Unity's board? What was I thinking? I sent him one final email letting him know how much it would mean to me and the organization at this critical stage of growth to have him involved.

I did not expect to hear back. Then I got a call from him directly. He told me that he hadn't replied because he was thinking about it and wanted to make sure he could deliver if he said yes. After our chat, he decided to join. I remember literally jumping up and down.

This showed me the power of asking for something even if I didn't think I was going to get it. I was always afraid to ask when I didn't think I deserved something, but this time I didn't back down, and I couldn't be more thankful. I am also very grateful to have made a dear friend who has mentored me in my professional and personal life. I learned a valuable lesson from this experience: *persistence is the key to growth*, and I should never feel badly for asking for what we need to move Unity forward.

GENUINE CONNECTIONS: CHAMPIONS OF YOUTH MENTAL HEALTH

In 2014 I did a keynote for a fundraising conference called D3, organized by a mentor of mine, Mark Hierlihy. I was the only person on the speakers lineup that had no real public profile. Other speakers on the roster included Susan McIsaac, the former CEO of United Way of Greater Toronto; Michael McCain, the CEO of Maple Leaf Foods; and David Johnston, the former Governor General of Canada. This was a huge opportunity for me to get the Unity story out in a big way. My bio on the conference website spoke to how our work supported youth empowerment and mental health. This resulted in a call from the governor general's staff to ask if the governor general's spouse, Her Excellency Sharon Johnston, could visit one of Unity's programs. I remember when I saw the caller ID on my phone before answering it read *Canada*. I stepped out of the meeting I was in as a call from Canada seemed like it could be important.

I was informed on the call that Sharon Johnston was very passionate about youth mental health. We invited her to our program at the Art Gallery of Ontario. Before arriving, the protocol was pretty intense. Her staff instructed me on the phone several times that I must address her as "Her Excellency."

I remember when she arrived, she burst through AGO's double doors wearing a snazzy pink leather blazer, with a glowing smile on her face. I stumbled on my first words as I uttered them: "Hi, Your . . . Excellency," and she promptly interrupted and exclaimed, "Don't be silly! Call me Sharon!" She insisted we call her by her first name, and the ice was broken. She has the biggest heart for young people and was so down to earth. We performed, youth shared their stories, she asked tons of questions, and we all connected on an authentic human level. She was so engaged that she ended up staying well over our scheduled time together, making her late for her next event. After this visit, she insisted we call her the "Unity Hip Hop Granny."

Only a few months later, the Johnstons came to visit our program in Halifax. They listened intently to our stories about using hip hop to overcome adversity and asked really thoughtful questions. A young person shared a spoken word poem that shook the room. We took in every word of Brandon MacDougall's poem with jaw-dropping awe, and it beautifully tied together everything Unity stood for in its closing line: "If arts were our only weapons, imagine how beautiful war could be."

We gave Unity sweaters to Sharon and David and told them they were now part of the Unity family. Not missing a beat, they put the sweaters on right over their dress clothes. I asked how we could remain in touch, and Sharon told me to apply for patronage. So we did, and the Johnstons became honourary patrons of Unity. In 2015 they asked me to be their guest to the Speech from the Throne. They invited me to stay over for two nights at "RH," which is how they referred to Rideau Hall in their email. It was an incredible experience to learn more about Canada and about how government works firsthand from the representatives of the Queen.

I was surprised to wake up on that first morning at RH and be invited to have breakfast with them (and their dog Rosie). It was a bit overwhelming and truly humbling. I learned that regardless of what position of power you hold, you can always have humility, be generous and authentic. I also learned that our system of government and really any role can be transformational if you navigate it with your authentic voice. We can help get the arts, mental health, and hip hop to a much larger stage for impact if we have the right advocates. David and Sharon used their roles to do so much good for the world, it was a true honour to get to know them.

Flipping Outreach: Hip Hop on the Hill

This ridiculously awesome snowball of one major opportunity leading to another taught me about the power of a pitch from the stage. The stage became the most impactful place to pitch our ideas. Getting even five minutes to speak at major events essentially became a way to build mass awareness in new audiences. It was our way in the door. We had a backstage pass to people we could never have met otherwise. This taught me to seek connectors who could introduce me to new people and platforms to share our story. Give me fifteen minutes at your biggest conference to share what Unity does, and I promise we'll energize the crowd with a powerful and inspiring hip hop performance. We called these Unity Blitz Performances, and over the years they've gotten us in front of hundreds of thousands of people. These performances directly connected us to new supporters, funders, and internal advocates for our cause.

In the fall of 2016, the Unity fundraising crew, including Rajni, Kevin, and me, decided to do a government outreach tour in Ottawa. We hired a government PR organization to help us set up meetings with people who could help us get funding and went to Ottawa to do over eighteen meetings in three days. By the end of it all, we thought we were going to faint from running around and repeating the same message. We built some great relationships with federal MPs with the goal to advocate for government funding for our programs. We called it Hip Hop on the Hill and did it the Unity way: we did a dance performance in an MP's office, taking handshake photos in breakin' freezes, and I wore sweaters with fish and fox cartoons on them. We shared our story our way and built strong government allies.

Unity wasn't trying to build partnerships with folks who didn't directly align with our values, and the only way of testing that out was to fully express who we are in every interaction with potential supporters. This helped attract the right supporters. It was like we were putting out a magnetic force and seeing who got pulled in.

I remember walking by the office of an MP whose name we recognized. We went into the office and said to the secretary at the front desk, "Please say hi to Marco Mendocino for us. He came out to speak at our event last week after presenting a cheque for one of our largest ever grants from Canadian Heritage." She replied, "He isn't in right now, but I will pass along the message. Why are you in Ottawa? Are you doing government lobbying?"

I paused, like a deer in headlights, looked at my colleagues and awkwardly replied, "I don't . . . think . . . so . . . ?" She then replied, "Government lobbying isn't a bad thing." And I said, "Well, then, I guess we are doing that." We all laughed. For some reason, "government lobbying" sounded scary to me, but apparently that was exactly what we were doing.

Funnily enough, not only did Marco come to our event earlier that year to speak, but on the way to our event he wrote a spoken word poem that he performed in front of all of Unity's supporters. He was a great sport and made that event a lot of fun. Marco is another person in a position of power who shared himself with Unity in a genuine way, breaking down power dynamics and making government more accessible. Being in a position of power is an incredible opportunity to welcome people into your home and open real doors of opportunity. It all started by putting our true selves out into the world and seeing who was magnetized to connect.

One day I got an email from an insurance company that wanted to book Unity to perform at its national sales conference. We were advised that there wasn't a large budget, so our payment would have to be earned through donations from employees plus a small honorarium to pay our artists. We were a bit hesitant, so we negotiated that the company would match up to five thousand dollars in donations made by employees that night and agreed to do the gig on these terms. The party was thrown at a big nightclub in Toronto.

When employees arrived at the venue at 7:00 p.m., I was sitting at a table at the entrance with a box that had the words *donation box* written in bubble letters with a red marker. After around one hundred people passed me without making a donation, I decided to not stand there any longer. This clearly wasn't working so I left the box, hoping someone might make an example by putting in a twenty-dollar bill.

We had Unity DJ and staffer Andel play the party, and everyone was dancing up a storm. Finally, at 10:00 p.m. Unity was given the stage for a fifteen-minute Blitz performance. I took the microphone and asked everyone to form a circle. There must have been four hundred people in the room. I shared the story of how we started Unity and the impact we had across Canada. Then we did a beatboxing and dancing showcase where I also threw down with the crew. One of their employees shocked us when they jumped in the circle and started breakin'. The crowd went wild. As we performed, we had Jessey painting graffiti on a massive canvas, and the employees could tag their name on the piece that read "big, bold, brave." At the end of the performance, I pitched from the stage and asked everyone to donate personally so their company would match donations up to five thousand dollars.

After our performance, Andel took over. Suddenly an older gentleman interrupted and asked for the mic. I ran up to the stage as I thought something was wrong. He began to shout, "On behalf of Western Canada, our team wants to donate three thousand dollars to Unity, and we are challenging everyone in the room to beat us!" All of a sudden groups in the room began to get into huddles and whisper. It appeared insurance professionals don't joke around when it comes to competition.

Next a woman came up on stage and said, "On behalf of the Quebec region's team, we would like to donate forty-five hundred dollars!" Everyone roared in applause. The huddles reformed. Finally another woman in high heels came up to the stage, grabbed the mic and shouted, "Your donations are as low as your sales! On behalf of the Toronto team, we are going to donate six thousand dollars!" Donations rolled in for the rest of the night.

I couldn't believe it! By the end of the night, we had raised over eighteen thousand dollars in individual donations from one performance! The head office folks got on stage because they felt badly for only offering five thousand dollars in matching donations and announced they would match the full amount that employees donated. Unity raised over thirty-six grand in one night!

When we first got booked for this event, I didn't even want to do it because it felt like just another event where we would walk away barely able to pay our artists. I was shockingly wrong. We took a chance, gave that fifteen minutes our all, and it became the first of many stories like this.

BUILD A NETWORK OF CHAMPIONS

When I broke the news that I was leaving Unity, one by one artists shared personal stories of the impact Unity'd had in their lives. One of the youth alumni from the program who was now on Unity's artist roster said that one of the gifts I had was "weaving a spider web of unlikely champions" for the cause. He was speaking to the fact that I engaged people from different backgrounds, beliefs, and experiences to come together and support our cause.

I was building a network of Unity champions. Over my fifteen years there, I made it my mission to meet as many people as I could from different roles, backgrounds, and experiences. I was spreading our work by giving people my time, no matter their job title or where they came from. I met with community organizations, artists, school officials, funders, program alumni, and really anyone who reached out to me with an interest in getting involved with or supporting Unity's mission. People from multiple sectors and experiences heard our story, and I listened to theirs. We figured out how to work together and support one another. If we couldn't find a way to work together, at least we were now aware of each other's work in the bigger picture. We were constantly learning about the larger ecosystem we were part of, so we became more efficient in not duplicating efforts. Exchanging ideas is the heart of my approach to effective collaboration and community building. We can't solve today's biggest and most pressing social challenges in silos. I believed it was my responsibility to know what was going on.

Unity's reputation, network, and mentors created a solid foundation. I personally had a list of over twenty-five hundred people I met over the fifteen years it took to build Unity, whom I'd kept in touch with about major developments in our organization. Each person was like a brick, carefully laid, that led to a house after fifteen years with a stable foundation. This did not happen overnight. Over the years, if anyone ever wanted to have a meeting with me, I would always make the time. I made sure that I gave anyone who spent time with me my full respect, energy, and attention. Even if these meetings didn't result in any kind of support, my goal was that every single person I met walked away feeling energized and respected.

My dad told me that one time someone asked him for job references when he was later in his career. He gave this person his entire phonebook of hundreds of contacts and permission to call anyone they wanted. I definitely learned this from my dad. I gave myself generously and openly. Sometimes meetings would go on for two hours. I would always learn something new, make a new connection, or build a new ally. Sometimes I even drove across the city and back for meetings when I had no idea if they would produce any results. My team always told me to stop wasting my time, but I couldn't deny people when they asked me to meet with them. These meetings helped grow a robust network of supporters that ultimately made Unity a more stable organization.

Flipping Leadership: Context Is Critical — Explore Your Ecosystem!

Leaders need to be aware of the external environment in which they operate. Each organization's context is different and often shifting, so it would be irresponsible not to pay attention to the environment around you when building and growing a social purpose organization. If you don't become aware of what is around you, then you could very well create an organization with the exact same goals and focus as another organization only a few blocks away.

I pushed myself to step outside of my comfort zone to keep a pulse on what was happening around us and in the wider non-profit ecosystem. There are so many people and organizations doing good work, but we don't leave our own office often enough. We need to build bridges across sectors. Being aware of who is taking action and what is actually happening in the community is a largely overlooked resource. There is so much untapped opportunity for doing better, but it is easier to just follow what others do, protect our slice of the pie, and connect the dots of what is familiar around us.

I was all about understanding the ecosystem we were part of and breaking down silos by bringing people together who do not normally come together in the same room for the same purpose. For example, Unity was created in a room full of youth, hip hop artists, students, community organizations, and working professionals. Digging deep into understanding the context in which we operate is critical when aiming to create responsible and sustainable impact.

ALWAYS A STUDENT

I was constantly looking for opportunities to learn. In 2015, I applied for a scholarship to attend Harvard University's Strategic Non-Profit Management Executive Education program. It was one of those applications I forgot about on purpose after I submitted it, because I didn't feel I deserved this opportunity. The program was super-competitive, and it seemed like only applicants from bigger organizations received this honour. Plus, it was Harvard. What b-boy is going to be accepted to Harvard?

I was overwhelmed when I found out I had been shortlisted. I went for an interview and was super nervous. I felt I had responded thoughtfully to the interviewer's questions, but I wanted to temper my expectations, so I just went back to work and focused on continuing to build Unity. Several weeks later I got a call from the interview committee. I remember exactly where I was when it came: walking past the Eaton Centre in downtown Toronto, in the rain, on my way to work. The person at the other end of the line said, "You are accepted into the program. Congratulations." I remember bursting out in tears in complete disbelief. I immediately called my Grampa. I knew in my heart he was the first person I wanted to tell. He was very traditional. I always wanted to make him proud, but he never told me he was. He always asked me, "When are you going to get into business and make money?"

When I called him to share the news about Harvard, it was the first time he told me he was proud of me. I could hear him smiling as he uttered the words. His grandson was going to Harvard. I received a scholarship to go, all expenses paid, to one of the most prestigious universities in the world. From a high school class project to Harvard. I looked at this honour as a major responsibility not only to learn, but to share my knowledge with others who may never get this opportunity. I cleared my schedule in preparation, so I could be a complete sponge and soak everything in. I felt like a tadpole in the ocean.

I read over three hundred pages of case studies before I even arrived at Harvard, and once I was there I took notes methodically. I wanted to be on top of this once-in-a lifetime opportunity to get the most out of it. I took over forty pages of notes in the lectures. At the end of each day, I summarized them into key learnings by topic so I could share them with my team and other non-profit leaders. The days were intense with over twelve hours of learning and collaborating with classmates. One of my fellow students told me, "It was like drinking from a firehose" — the perfect way to describe the experience. It was a ton to absorb in a very short period of time. Even though I was representing one of the smallest organizations in the program, I began to feel accepted as I realized that we were dealing with similar challenges in different cultural and geographic contexts.

Post-program, I shared notes, frameworks, and takeaways by topic with a few sector leaders that I respect in Toronto. I encouraged others to apply to the course. I kept in touch with several classmates when I needed advice or an outside eye on a specific issue. I joined the Harvard Business School Toronto chapter scholarship nominating committee to review applications and identify emerging and diverse leaders to participate in this incredible opportunity. I felt it was my responsibility to share access to this hard-to-reach sector knowledge. We used frameworks from the program to brainstorm strategic decisions at Unity staff retreats. There was so much value to be harnessed, but such a big barrier to entry for the average grassroots social impact leader.

At Harvard, I met leaders of organizations and social enterprises that I would *never* have come across otherwise. There were incredible leaders doing unbelievable social impact projects from all across the globe. My network, knowledge, and cohort of sector mentors expanded greatly. One of the people who interviewed me in the final stages of the selection process for the scholarship, Beth Horowitz, former CEO of American Express in Canada, ended up joining our board soon after I got back from Harvard, after I recommended her to Adam and the board nominations committee. Beth was incredibly generous in her work with non-profits. She is super knowledgeable about governance, she was passionate about Unity's mission, and I just knew she would be a perfect fit to help take the Unity board to the next level.

INVEST IN RELATIONSHIPS

Unity's growing network with key connectors joining the movement created a much better chance of sustainability. We were not a "big brand," but people began to recognize our name. The network at Unity eventually grew so large that when we met new potential supporters, often they said they had heard of us in some way. They would usually say something along the lines of, "I hear you do good work." Positive word-of-mouth became our most valuable asset.

Investing in relationships has connected me to the most amazing mentors and Unity champions. They have given me strategic guidance, provided an ear to listen, and opened major doors of opportunity. You never know when your network is advocating for you behind the scenes in conversations, at decision making tables, and in the community. As we grew, this happened often. Because of word of mouth and internal advocates, we even received funding we hadn't applied for. Our small snowball was now growing as it rolled down a big hill. We were gaining momentum and learning to harness this positive energy.

Networks are powerful if nurtured authentically and intentionally. They helped make us aware of potential partnerships that could add deeper impact to our cause. It's how we learned about Second Harvest to provide free healthy food and snacks in our after-school programs. It's how we connected to Nexus Youth Services to provide mental health support directly in our Mississauga hub programs. It is how we met Boost Child and Youth Advocacy Centre, who helped us secure over $1.4 million in government funding over five years to launch a trauma-informed dance therapy program. It's how we got featured as one of the first Canadian organizations on the Mental Health Innovation Network, based on a recommendation from the governor general.

Networks are nothing without a strong reputation built on hard work, honesty, and transparency. Unity became the group that many talked about positively when we were not in the room. The only way to get this type of reputation is to build it, slowly and over time, by meeting everyone open to supporting and inspiring them to get involved. I met Adam Silver, Unity's fourth board chair, at a wine and cheese networking event. He told me he was into hip hop when he grew up, and that sparked a conversation. If I'd never met him in this awkward moment, Unity never would have had such an amazing board chair several years later. I always opened myself to connecting authentically with outside supporters, and that led to many of Unity's biggest opportunities. We had to put ourselves out there to build new networks.

Beware Hidden Agendas

One experience taught me a lot about being careful in selecting mentors and volunteers. In 2011 we met a consultant who agreed to "volunteer" their time to help us evaluate our national programs. This consultant gave their time for a few months but never fully completed the job they were working on. When we asked the individual to complete it, we were told we would have to pay. It felt like we had been manipulated a bit, but we really wanted to complete this project, so we tried to find some funding to complete the job. We found a private foundation that enabled us to engage the consultant on an ongoing basis. The consultant's moves felt a bit sneaky, but we found two years of funding to get evaluation, coaching, and frontline support.

The consultant held long meetings with each member of our team, and those were beginning to stretch the capacity of our frontline staff and artists. The team was asked to get youth to fill out long and complicated surveys, do multiple focus group interviews, write extra summary reports, and even interview community partners. This process began to negatively affect the program flow. There was just too much to do, and it was unclear how the results were going to be helpful or useful. The team began to push back. They told me the meetings and new evaluation processes were straining their already limited bandwidth. The consultant did not have the soft skills to truly listen to our team and develop healthy working relationships with them. Ultimately they did not appreciate how overworked the frontline staff were.

The consultant was just there to do their job no matter how they got it done. By not communicating empathetically with our team and not truly listening and adapting evaluations to best fit Unity's culture, the consultant became a barrier to success and was taking away from the program team's ability to do their job. This was the line for us. It became so disruptive that we needed to let this consultant go. We told them it just wasn't a fit.

I learned that not all mentors are good mentors. I became wary of "volunteers" who had hidden agendas to upsell their services. I needed to vet potential conflicts of interest or harmful egos when working with anyone volunteering their expertise to Unity. Although these situations were very rare, we needed to make sure that the volunteering had no strings attached. We learned from this experience and leveled up our processes to onboard volunteers and feel out potential mentors to better understand their true motivations and intentions before engaging with them.

THE POWER OF A GOOD REPUTATION

One day we received a cheque for eighteen thousand dollars from the Toronto Foundation, and naturally we were over the moon with joy. I would always do a happy dance when we got a big cheque in the mail. I asked the fundraising team who had applied for this grant, and much to my surprise, they said none of them had. I became worried that they had sent us a cheque by mistake. No one would send eighteen grand without having received an application or having been asked for that money. Even though it would be nice to cash this cheque, I had to be honest and tell Toronto Foundation they had made a mistake. I called them and they said, "It wasn't a mistake. Someone from our foundation recommended you to a private donor internally, as they knew about the great work you do." I felt joy mixed with confusion. This *never* happens in real life. Wait, maybe this is a weird dream. I always have weird dreams of Unity getting unexpected cheques in the mail. I pinched myself. Nope. This was real.

I thought, we don't deserve this, but we actually really need it. We had built a great relationship with the staff at the foundation, and because we were on their mind as a high-impact organization, they had recommended us for this sizable donation out of nowhere. This showed me the power and importance of a reputation. We have continued to receive this same grant for over five years and even increased the donation from eighteen thousand to sixty-five thousand dollars per year! People talking behind your back, in a good way, is something we strive to amplify.

RESOURCES VS. RESOURCEFULNESS

I believe in being resourceful in every way possible. I asked my friend Julian Van Mil, who makes television commercials, to help us create five different TV spots to promote Unity's cause. He very generously donated his services completely in-kind. These were top-quality productions filmed with Red cameras, one of the highest-quality cameras on the market, and unbelievable custom-designed 3D animation. Because our commercials were so cool, we were able to get the airtime on thirty national TV channels donated for several years for free as well. The commercials aired across the country even during prime time and March

Madness! This was an extraordinary gift with major value. We got it because we asked. Rajni was key in leading this pitch and the growth of our relationships with Bell Canada, Much Music, and MTV Canada. I think it's silly for charities to spend big money on national advertising, so we asked and got it for free. In 2012, Julian also donated his time to design Unity's logo. He was incredibly generous in supporting our cause. Resourcefulness is something we don't spend enough time thinking about. How can we get something of great value for free?

Our strategy for securing in-kind support started by looking at our budget and asking "Who in our network can help us save money?" We would then attempt to cut any budget item we could by tapping into our networks. Over the years we were able to cut multiple costs from food in programs to vital organizational services. We got free pizza for programs, free legal services to create staff contracts, free HR advice, free printed banners for our festival, free advertising on big billboards, and free soap (yes, soap). We gave the soap away in gift bags at our donor engagement events, and people loved it. We tried to get anything we could get for free that was useful to move our mission forward or build the organization. Eventually we were saving over forty thousand dollars each year from donations of products and services. We even received over twenty thousand dollars' worth of DJ and music equipment for our programs from the TD MusiCounts Program, affiliated with the JUNO Awards, including several sets of DJ turntables, mixers, beat looping pedals, wireless microphones, and multiple speakers. When a full in-kind donation wasn't possible, we asked for, and often got, discounts from most major suppliers. We also looked at donations other charities received: we would ask around and then try to secure similar items in-kind.

We also got free radio ads and digital billboards at Yonge-Dundas Square and in airports across the country, which created significant awareness for our holiday donation campaigns in a way that we could never have afforded. We even got people to donate their unused Aeroplan miles to Unity so we could exchange them for discounted flights and hotels to reduce our travel expenses for our national programming. The value of these in-kind donations was probably worth more than our entire annual operating budget.

One major expense we saw a few strategic charities get donated was office space. We were never successful securing office space, but that didn't stop us from trying. There were certain high-cost items we tried to get donated for years, and eventually our perseverance paid off. We had to be resourceful and save money wherever we could. We were conscious however not to take advantage of those who donated their services. We focused our asks of in-kind support on those who had healthy profit margins often in the corporate sector. In this way, Unity was able to sustain its work while still paying people fairly and respecting their time.

SPEAK TRUTH TO FUNDERS

The toughest conversations I had to have while building Unity were with funders when their actions, policies, and practices were, intentionally or unintentionally, making it more difficult for us to deliver programs to the very communities they sought to serve. There is an obvious tension here. If I speak my mind about a situation I see as detrimental or harmful, then Unity's funding might be cut off. At one end of the spectrum, there were requirements tied to applications, use of funds, and reporting that would take time and resources on the part of the non-profit — which in turn limited the support that could be given to communities in need. At the other end of the spectrum were less benign behaviours including a lack of respect for privacy, insensitive language, inaccessible reporting structures, and a failure to respect a community's right to define its own areas of need.

After a few years of developing a stable pool of donors and funders, I began to have direct conversations with funders about the importance around the language, processes, and reporting structures that are often imposed on non-profits by funders. I brought them along in the conversation in a respectful manner, while at the same time making it very clear that these sensitivities were critical to discuss when working with vulnerable communities. I did this keeping in mind that funders have their own internal goals and very real external pressure to be accountable for the dollars they spend.

Some funders were open to having a respectful discussion on this topic, and some really did not welcome it. I had a funder once say to us, "Is that how you speak to someone who gives you money?" The answer is yes. If the money is for the purpose of having an impact in a community and the actions of the funder are limiting or restricting this impact, the funder needs to know this. I believed it was my responsibility to let funders know that their actions — their rules, ways of communicating, and choices around priorities, evaluation, and reporting — have impact. We had to partner with funders while at the same time advocating for the communities we served. By having these tough conversations, we were trying to make things better for the wider non-profit ecosystem.

Nowadays funders are tightening up their funding guidelines as they receive lots of pressure to be more accountable to the public and to several bottom lines. As a result, charities are forced to jump through more hoops to access fewer funds. It's a vicious cycle, and it's only getting worse. Every time a funder would set an unrealistic expectation of us, I'd speak to the person responsible and explain to them the impact it was having on our organization and, indirectly, on the communities we served. Some didn't like me after these conversations, but others would welcome the opportunity to improve their processes. I felt like I was advocating for a larger purpose, and if we lost our funding as a result of these candid conversations, then our values had not been aligned with that particular funder to begin with.

There was one funder with whom we were building a great relationship. They had a rule that they could only fund a new program at organizations once every three years. I thought this was silly, because it was not realistic to start a program and put it on pause for two years until they could fund it again. On a positive note, all levels of the organization expressed support for what Unity was doing and how they felt a partnership would be a great fit. We decided to arrange a call with their community investment manager to ask if we could get around these rules or if they could change them, because otherwise they were putting the program at risk. We might as well not start a new program if we know we are going to be closing it down the following year.

At the last minute, I could not attend the phone call, so I asked our lead fundraiser to do so on my behalf. She'd been in many meetings when we'd had similar conversations, so I had full confidence that she could handle it. A few hours later she called, very upset, because the funder had scolded and criticized her for speaking up and advocating for continued funding over the full three years. The funder had literally bullied us. I was so mad I could barely hold back. I also felt terrible that I'd put my colleague in this position.

A few months earlier, that same funder had come to our office with an oversized fake cheque to take a picture with their leadership team so they could brag about their gift to Unity on social media. Thinking back on that, I knew I needed to report this incident. I sent a letter to the COO of the company about what had happened. I was very direct. A few days later, I received a phone call from the COO. He had listened, and he apologized. He said he would deal with it.

Even with the apology, we never worked with that funder again. We need to step up and speak out in our sector about these moments and let people know they can't push others around just because they are the ones holding the purse strings. In fact, these folks should be the ones going out of their way to involve community, be empathetic, and truly listen. Because we unfailingly spoke our truth, we were able to align with funders who shared our values while pushing away funders who were in it for the wrong reasons or not aligned with Unity's values. We were also able to advocate for several funders to change their guidelines, reporting structures, and processes for working with charities.

This is a note to all funders out there to be better listeners, involve the communities you seek to serve, reflect on the impact of your day-to-day interactions, and check your privilege. We need to all step up to the plate in equal partnership, with humility, and with community need at the forefront of our conversations. I think Spider-Man's Uncle Ben said it best: "With great power comes great responsibility."

THE EVOLUTION OF UNITY PROGRAMS

Over the years, Unity programs evolved as we saw new ways hip hop could empower youth, give them an outlet for their stress and a powerful voice in front of their peers, and help them build resilience. It all started with us doing inspirational performance-based assemblies in schools in underserved and marginalized communities in 2004. These assemblies had five of Unity's artists from the various hip hop art forms that Unity taught: breakin', beatboxing, spoken word poetry, MCing, and graffiti art. We created a skit that the artists would act out that allowed them to play different characters in a high school, showing their experiences using their art form to express their stress and build community. The skit was co-written by a cultural innovator and awesome Toronto playwright, Ravi Jain. The skit included Unity artists sharing their art and had sections they could freestyle and integrate messages as well as humour that was relevant to their personality and their story. After each scene, the artists would step out of character and share their personal stories. This was a huge part of Unity. Our work needed to be engaging, relevant, and real.

We would find out in advance some of the issues the students were dealing with, whether it was violence, bullying, mental health, a recent suicide, or other loss in the community. The artists would share different parts of their stories to help connect with the youth in a genuine way. We did everything we could in this one-hour show to break down barriers, talk openly about relevant issues, and build trust among youth in the high schools we worked in.

The relationships in the work we did were vital. We encouraged teachers to build stronger relationships with students who they were struggling to engage through Unity's programs. We were helping make school more relevant and engaging youth in genuine ways into life, education, and their own mental health. We also would get students in the school to perform and share their own stories through performances to help bring in an even more community-engaged, youth-led message. This took a ton of courage from the students who performed in these assemblies. Oftentimes we had youth perform for the first time ever and step out of their comfort zone in ways that shocked their teachers, peers, and even themselves. There were many powerfully positive moments we witnessed in these performances where youth would redefine their social image in one performance. They were truly heard and the ripple effect lived on. Eventually we took this idea for these one-off shows and created Unity Days. Unity Days was a program that took the five-artist assembly with student performances and expanded it into a full-day program.

After the assembly, we would run a cypher in a busy hallway in the school. This would often attract a ton of attention, often from the kids in the school who were hanging out in the hallways already, sometimes skipping class. At first, people would gather in a circle thinking a fight might break out, but then would realize it was a beatboxing, dance, and rap cypher and join in. We would invite and encourage students in the school to jump in the cypher and share anything they liked, as long as it was appropriate for the school environment. After the cypher we would have our artist educators visit classrooms. We would have graffiti artists take over art class, spoken word artists take over English class, beatboxers take over music or math class, and dancers take over gym class. The goal was to have artists give students an opportunity to experience a new outlet for their stress and to help them build the courage to be vulnerable in front of their peers and express themselves.

Unity Days became the spark. They got youth to engage in all of the other programs that Unity offered. Eventually we would use Unity Days to launch and promote our after-school programs. The after-school program started as a twelve-week program that we eventually expanded to happen across the entire school year from September to June. This program helped youth step through different lessons in various hip hop art forms that were all themed around different elements of building resilience, leadership skills, and mentorship. These lesson plans were co-created by program coordinators and artist educators to ensure they were engaging, relevant, and adaptable. The after-school program ended with youth performing a themed piece for their school, creating a huge graffiti mural in their community, and teaching their newfound skills to youth in the feeder elementary schools. Over the years, we added different elements to the after-school programs to enhance them, like t-shirts when participants graduated, food to keep them energized, journals to document parts of their journeys, connection pathways to other Unity programs, referrals to community partners, and much more.

Healing through Hip Hop

Stephen "Buddha" Leafloor, has been a close mentor and friend since Unity began. Buddha is an old school b-boy, a social worker, and the founder of BluePrintForLife and Blueprint Pathways, intensive hip hop mental health programs in remote Indigenous communities, alternative schools, and youth detention centres . Buddha hired me in 2009 as a breakin' facilitator on his team for several week-long projects in remote Arctic communities and youth detention centres.

Being a part of the transformative impact on the Blueprint team expanded my belief in what is possible through hip hop outreach. Buddha's programs changed young people's lives, in communities with alarmingly high rates of suicide, drug and alcohol addiction, and serious mental illness. The Blueprint program takes over an entire week of school with hip hop and deep talks around issues facing communities. Buddha calls it "Social work through hip hop."

The days were long and intense, and the relationships built led to breakthroughs in healing for everyone involved, even the teachers in the schools and local police. We would often go on projects with up to ten hip hop artists all bringing unique gifts to the work with the kids. Buddha became a mentor to several Unity staff and artists who became staff on Blueprint projects.

Going on Blueprint projects was one of the best professional development experiences I ever had. Every time someone came back from their first Blueprint project, their views would often change on how much of an impact hip hop can truly have. It also gave artists space to explore their own personal healing and trauma.

On these week-long projects, we lived together, flew in tiny airplanes, cooked together, explored the land together, and had each other's back. Buddha led intensive talks on serious issues including trauma, mental health, drugs, alcohol abuse, and healing. By the end of the week, youth performed in front of their entire community and were celebrated for their successes. As a team, Blueprint had a ton of fun on projects. To get initiated into the Blueprint family, I did snow angels in my underwear in −40° temperatures and even swam in the Arctic Ocean off the coast of Nunavut in −25° cold. We had a lot of fun and expanded our knowledge on ways hip hop can heal.

We eventually created funded partnerships between Unity and Blueprint and shared training resources including a cultural exchange program funded by the Ontario Trillium Foundation called Share Our Spirit (SOS). SOS was an exchange between youth in Unity after-school programs and youth living in remote Arctic communities. Buddha also shared his codes of conduct for working with youth with the Unity team as he had lots of knowledge in this area from his experience as a social worker. Buddha truly embodies the "each one teach one" mindset of hip hop and continues to pass down knowledge to the next generation of hip hoppers and outreach workers worldwide.

After a few years of expanding Unity Days to launch after-school programs in underserved communities across the Greater Toronto Area, we eventually brought this work to other provinces across Canada, including Alberta, Nova Scotia, New Brunswick, British Columbia, and Manitoba. This eventually evolved into Unity's national programs where in each community we found local organizations to partner with, did outreach visits to build relationships, and sought local funding to support ongoing programs there. We would also train local artist educators under Unity's model.

A huge part of Unity's secret sauce was in how we trained our frontline artist educators. This was vital to Unity's success. Over the years Unity trained over 250 artists across the country on how to be effective and engaging artist educators. We taught them everything from how to share their personal stories in ways that are relatable and safe to what are the Unity codes of conduct of appropriate ways of working with youth. We also had our top artists document their "magic" and how they engaged youth. Documenting this process allowed us to codify this magic to eventually invite youth from our programs to get trained to join Unity's artist roster. Unity strived for full circle impact through mentorship. The artist training program was held as a three-day retreat where we brought artists into the wilderness and gave them training on what it took to be an effective Unity artist educator. We eventually followed up with additional training that supplemented this retreat, including onboarding, annual update trainings, and specialized certifications.

We were really intense and serious about our quality standards for artist educators, and this was baked in to how we ran our training. As part of the retreat, we had a surprise wakeup call at 5:00 a.m. to get everyone to go for a run in the woods. If one person was late we made everyone wait for them, sometimes in the freezing cold. I remember one morning we had twenty artists waiting for one artist who took their time to get up in -30° weather. We wanted to demonstrate that if you are late for a school program or assembly, then you truly let your whole team down. Solidarity was vital as we could not run our programs and let down the youth. If one artist is late and lets down a youth in our after-school programs, that youth may never attend a program again. This to us was serious, and we did not accept lateness. At Unity, if you were early, you were on time. Eventually the Unity artist educator roster was so strong — we even had artists that had been with us for over a decade. We began to have different levels, from senior artists to professional artist to emerging artist to youth mentors.

At a final event we called the Unity Kickoff Concert, youth from different schools would come together to share their stories and skills in front of youth from other communities, backgrounds, and experiences. We would invite parents, teachers, and community members to celebrate the youth in the Kickoff. As part of the show, youth competed for a one-time scholarship to support their future artistic development. Eventually we decided to expand this event and booked the largest public venue in the City of Toronto — Yonge-Dundas Square in the heart of downtown. We also got government grants from the Department of Canadian Heritage and the Ontario Arts Council to book a major international headliner. This was a big deal for the youth because they were sharing the stage with their hip hop heroes. Over the years, we were able to get top international artists such as Talib Kweli, Biz Markie, GZA, Rahzel, Kardinal Offishall, Maestro Fresh Wes, Dam Funk, Monte Booker, and Michie Mee. We renamed the event Unity Festival and grew it into a four-day festival that had a different day dedicated to each of the art forms that Unity taught: graffiti art, spoken word poetry, breakin', and beatboxing.

Eventually we realized we could have a different, yet important impact outside of schools. We tested what we called "community programs" that were held in community partner spaces and community centres. We noticed there was a gap. There were so many physical spaces in priority neighbourhoods across the GTA; however, they often struggled to provide consistent, high-quality arts programs that were relatable and engaging to youth. In Unity's community programs, youth could learn more deeply about each of the art forms Unity taught.

In the spaces outside of the schools, we often attracted youth who were a bit older, often between the ages of seventeen and twenty-four, whereas in our after-school program students were mostly twelve to seventeen years old. We began to offer more community programs as we realized youth also have a different way of being outside of school. They often felt more open to share their stories in our spoken word programs and express themselves in different ways then they could in school. Both programs were different in age range and had different expected outcomes in our theory of change based on the advantages that both school spaces and community spaces offered. We also had different artist educators who worked better in schools and some who engaged better with youth in community settings. We continued to refine, learn, and test new elements to increase the quality and outreach of Unity's community programs. Through partnerships with local community organizations, social service agencies, and other referrals in the mental health space, we were able to provide different community programs that appealed to different youth, artists, and communities. Our programs were adaptable in a variety of contexts.

We also developed a strong pool of volunteers over the years as the festival needed over one hundred volunteers each year. They were trained by our amazing volunteer coordinators, Karen Au and Kieon Bisnath. Our volunteers also helped sell Unity Shop clothing as a mini social enterprise. Over the years Unity Shop was co-created, designed, and run by several artists and even youth alumni including CG Chen, Jim Cartasano, Shamar Ramsay, and eventually Diamond Osoteo. They each added their own unique contribution of fashion design, connected to Unity values. We told anyone who put on a Unity Shop piece of clothing that when you wear anything with the Unity logo you live our values of respect, passion, integrity, and community. This meant you couldn't go to a party wearing a Unity shirt and do things you shouldn't be doing. It was a constant reminder to live with strong values in the decisions you make. Volunteers helped us get more t-shirts to more youth across Canada.

We even had youth alumni register Unity student clubs at four different universities across Ontario to continue to run on-campus hip hop workshops and events, source volunteers, and continue to engage youth who had graduated from our programs and gone on to university. These youth alumni also engaged the wider university student population who were dealing with their own stresses. Youth alumni started and maintained University chapters at York University, University of Toronto Scarborough campus, University of Toronto St. George campus, and University of Western Ontario. For those who didn't go on to university, we created an alumni program where we would gather alumni to socialize, network, and stay in touch. After over fifteen years, Unity had a wide network of youth who had grown up and some who came back to work with Unity as contract artist educators, and even a handful who were hired as full-time and part-time staff. We strongly believed in the full-circle approach to our work, providing employment and opportunities to share art and get paid to youth who had barriers to opportunities like this. Mentorship is a foundational value in hip hop, we tried to embody the "each one teach one" philosophy in our hiring practices.

All of Unity's programs eventually were framed in our theory of change. This was our North Star. Any program we ran had to focus on improving the mental health and well-being of youth aged twelve to twenty-four living in underserved communities. Youth would attend programs regularly and contribute to the well-being of their community through mentorship, performance, and volunteer opportunities provided by Unity. Over the years, Unity continued to evolve and adapt while responding to changing needs in the communities we served. We built an organization that was responsive and reliable for the youth we served.

1. Create a revenue pipeline and prospect list for your project/organization. (See sample template in the Tools & Resources section at the back of the book or visit epicleadership.ca/bookresources.)

    a. Try to rank and organize your list of potential funders based on fit for support, timing of funding, percent likelihood of receiving funding, and strategy for how you will get in front of them. (Include as much information as is relevant to best track your funders: contact details of grant officers, timing of applications, links to guidelines, focus areas, programs you think they might support, notes about relationship, and any categories you can track that are helpful to organizing your fundraising process.)

    b. Do your research: find grant databases, copy similar charity donor lists, ask your board, search LinkedIn, ask mentors / advisors, etc.

    c. Think about your ideal revenue split by program and by funding source (set percentages and dollar amounts per funding type as goals). How can you work towards achieving these goals with the support of your revenue pipeline?

2. How can you grow your list of warm leads to pitch for support? (Consider different categories of support from financial to in-kind, including individual donations, sponsors, government, corporate, foundations, event ticket sales, earned revenue, in-kind product/ service, third-party fundraisers, and any relevant revenue sources.)

3. Who are some of the biggest champions of your work? How can you get the most support from each champion in your network? How can you grow this list?

4. With which of your current funders can you grow their support? How would you go about growing these relationships and increasing your ask?
5. What unique ways can you engage your funders and partners? How can you stand out and customize your engagements to partner needs?
6. What in-kind products and services can you look for to reduce your costs? How can you be more resourceful in saving money without cutting quality?
7. How can storytelling and evaluation play a role in fundraising?

PART 5

EVOLVE
Steps to Succession

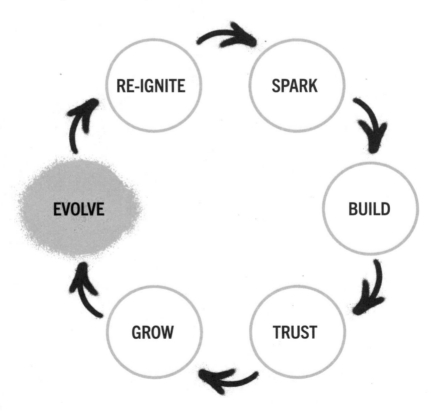

ON CHILDREN

Your children are not your children.
They are the sons and daughters of Life's longing for itself.
They come through you but not from you,
And though they are with you yet they belong not to you.

You may give them your love but not your thoughts,
For they have their own thoughts.
You may house their bodies but not their souls,
For their souls dwell in the house of tomorrow, which you cannot visit,
    not even in your dreams.
You may strive to be like them, but seek not to make them like you.
For life goes not backward nor tarries with yesterday.
You are the bows from which your children as living arrows are sent forth.
The archer sees the mark upon the path of the infinite, and He bends
    you with His might that His arrows may go swift and far.
Let your bending in the archer's hand be for gladness;

For even as He loves the arrow that flies, so He loves also the bow that
is stable.

— Khalil Gibran

REFLECTING ON LEADERSHIP: AT A CROSSROADS

I remember being in a Unity staff meeting and Cat, who was in charge
of Unity's community programs, told me about a training session she
had attended from a local community arts partner. SKETCH Working
Arts offered "artful anti-oppression" training for its staff and partners.
Cat suggested we bring this session to Unity. I told her I would check
the budget to see if we could make it happen. Cat has a ton of integrity.
Whenever she advocated for something, I knew it was worth looking
into. So we contacted Julian Diego and Naty Tremblay, facilitators from
SKETCH, and set up training for Unity staff and artists. What trans-
pired forced me to look within myself and explore my biases, privileges,
and ways of interacting with the world. It helped me reflect deeply on my
role and Unity's role when it comes to addressing power imbalance and
inequity. The best part was that SKETCH facilitated this all through art.

A few weeks following the training, I noticed my language shift
slightly. I was becoming more conscious of the space I took up in a way
I had never considered. It put me on a new path of self-learning. I was
a white, able-bodied, cisgender male running a hip hop organization for
youth facing multiple barriers I had never had to face myself. I had to
revisit my leadership. What was my role in the future of Unity? I didn't
have an answer. I just had a bunch of new questions. I explored the idea
that I didn't need to be at the front of the room all the time to make the
impact I wanted to have. What it took to build Unity might not be what
it needed going forward.

This self-reflection was a major part of my decision to leave Unity. If I wasn't able to push the organization, then my contribution would go stale. I had given everything I could give. The other major part of my decision had to do with my well-being.

IT'S OKAY TO NOT BE OKAY

I equated success with working my ass off. Driving with no brakes. I would have eight to twelve meetings every day, running across the city while still running the day-to-day operations of Unity. In a decade, I had sent over 426,808 emails! I would respond to emails within minutes, sometimes even seconds, of receiving them. I was the busiest person I knew, but I still made time for everyone and everything. It was exhausting, but the challenge to keep up was fuelled by pure adrenaline. I felt like nothing could stop me. It was like sprinting constantly in a race with no finish line. I worked relentlessly because I knew the idea of using hip hop to improve young people's lives was solid. I knew this was going to work — I just had to keep sprinting. I thought I could keep this pace forever and this endless sprint was what I attributed to Unity's success.

I realized that the stress that had been built up and bottled up over the years had literally caused me to have a mental health breakdown. At the age of thirty, I began to experience intense anxiety. My body was physically reacting to all the experiences I was holding onto throughout my childhood and life. I started to have crippling panic attacks that were leaving me confused and scared.

Admitting I had a mental health issue was one of the most difficult things for me. For some reason, I didn't want to say I had this "thing." When I was growing up, the stigma surrounding mental illness influenced me to never tell people about my mom's battle with schizophrenia, so I felt like I was supposed to hold it in. But I learned that it wasn't who

I was but was something I was experiencing. It did not define me, and I could work through it. This way of looking at it helped me down a path of seeking ongoing treatment to help me cope and become effective in work and life. I have friends who have had anxiety their whole life and never sought treatment. I did everything I could to get well and get back to work. I wanted to solve this, but this wasn't "solvable." I saw a psychologist, I began meditating, I began cutting down my schedule drastically, and I started to learn to live with anxiety. Carrying the weight of a mountain on my shoulders left a lasting impact on my mental health. I couldn't just walk it off or ignore it, I needed help.

My anxiety as a child, though, was in many ways the reason I found hip hop in the first place and the very reason that Unity was built — using hip hop as a catalyst to give other youth an outlet for their stress and anger. It was the perfect storm. Hip hop changed my life for the better, and did so for many of my close friends and crew. I knew I wanted to share this; it became my life's mission. However, in building Unity, I often neglected myself and my own mental health. I stopped doing the things that I needed to do to help myself, and in turn this led me again to a place of extremes.

My therapist brought to my attention that I often think in extremes. This has helped me make big decisions without looking back. However, it has also caused me to believe the world actually operates in extremes when, more often than not, it doesn't. I learned in therapy that Aristotle's golden mean is something I can remind myself of when I'm creating a "this" or "that" situation or story. The answer, the truth, is usually somewhere in the middle.

For example, what led me to developing a fear of flying when I experienced anxiety? My initial thought was something along the lines of, "If I fly in an airplane, I might die in a plane crash." I also worried if I had a panic attack on a long flight, I wouldn't be able to make it through the entire flight because I would be trapped. These thoughts led to me developing a fear of flying, and I would experience physical symptoms of anxiety from sweating to shaking before I boarded a plane. When the symptoms were bad, I missed flights.

The other extreme was to think, "I love flying because I can disconnect and get caught up on my sleep." I would be just trying to paint a rose-coloured picture to reduce my anxiety, which never really worked.

I had to reframe my thoughts to be more realistic, more along the lines of "I might get a stomachache or have a panic attack, but I'll get to where I'm going safely although a little stressed about the whole experience. I probably won't be able to sleep on a long flight, but I will try to watch a few movies to pass the time." I've been on hundreds of flights — and many long ones — since. After a bit of practice, reframing my thoughts to a more accurate representation of reality reduced my anxiety and physical symptoms associated with anxiety. I faced my fears and reframed exaggerated thoughts. It seems obvious, but I need to constantly remind myself of the golden mean to help focus on reality, which lies somewhere in the middle.

When my doctor told me I was experiencing anxiety, this was the first time I ever acknowledged I had a mental illness. Even though I used to hyperventilate as a child and get really bad stomach aches that would cause me to miss school, I never acknowledged that what I was going through was actually anxiety or a mental health condition. I just thought I was stressed out. I felt the right thing to do was notify Unity's board chair, Adam Silver, but I was so afraid to do this. I was essentially telling my boss I had a mental health issue. I remember thinking that however Adam responds will define how our organization, which focuses on supporting youth mental health, deals with our own employees' mental health issues. It all seemed a bit too ironic.

I was so worried that if he had a negative reaction to what I was going to tell him, I probably would have quit before he could fire me. It was a major, defining moment for me. Instead of thinking through every scenario in my head, I had to just pick up the phone. I remember having his number on my phone with my thumb hovering, ready but afraid to push call. Finally, I took a deep breath, closed my eyes, and pushed the call button. He answered right away, and I began explaining what I was feeling. Before I could finish my first sentence, I burst into tears on the phone. I wanted to hold it together, but I just couldn't, the anxiety was pumping through my body in that moment like a blazing fire. Even before hearing what he had to say I was already regretting calling as I broke down.

He calmly responded, "My only concern is ensuring you are okay."

The shame I had been feeling began to melt away. I'm honestly not sure what I expected; I just knew I had to tell him. I am so thankful for Adam and the values he holds as a leader and as a human being. He made me feel safe in one of my most vulnerable moments. I could see why most people never tell their bosses when they are battling mental health issues. It's beyond scary. Adam is not only my boss, but a great mentor and a true friend. He allowed me to lead by example, showing that it is okay to talk about our mental health in the work setting.

A week later, after checking up on me every single day by phone and even coming to visit me, Adam asked for my permission to tell the rest of the board of directors what was going on. I told him I was okay with this, and he sent an email to the board explaining what I was going through. Again, I held my breath anticipating what would happen next. I got a wave of positive support and genuine one-on-one catch-ups from the majority of board members. This showed me that we had created an institution that truly represented a culture supporting mental health at all levels of the organization. I felt deep pride about how this all unfolded. It greatly helped in my recovery to have such a supportive team around me.

I couldn't fulfil my responsibilities and missed many weeks of work. I just couldn't get through the day and face donors, supporters, or really anyone for that matter. I remember having an intense panic attack in the middle of a full-day strategic planning session with board and staff when presenting scenarios of the future national strategy. I didn't tell my team. Then another wave of guilt hit me. My staff began asking where I was and what was going on. I really didn't want to lie to them. At first, I told them I was sick. This made me feel even worse. I felt like I was lying even though technically I wasn't. I was sick — I just didn't have a cold.

Telling the staff was pivotal for me, although extremely difficult. I wanted to let them know that it is okay to talk about our mental health openly. After a few weeks, I had told a few key people on the team, but I still felt like everyone needed to know what was going on. I didn't want this to be a big secret or become some kind of rumour at the office. I wanted to lead by example and show them that our organization supports their mental health, and we can talk openly. I wanted to let them know that this organization supports them no matter the circumstance. So, I prepared to tell the entire team at the next staff meeting what I was going through. I didn't get a wink of sleep the night before.

Coincidentally, the ice breaker for that week's staff meeting was, "How are you dealing with your own self-care?" I think Rajni set this up on purpose as she wanted to create a positive space for me to share. I saw this as a great moment to let people know that I was battling anxiety. I told everyone and again burst into tears and felt an immediate wave of support. Over the next few days, my vulnerability made others feel safe enough to tell me what they were going through. I realized I made it okay to not be okay all the time, even if you're in a leadership role. I soon learned how many people deal with anxiety, depression, and all sorts of invisible illnesses that they never talk about. Whatever fear I felt telling the board, I realized my team was also in fear of telling me or anyone for that matter. This broke down so many walls I didn't even know existed.

In some ways I've looked at this whole experience as a really painful blessing in disguise. When the anxiety was the most intense, and I didn't know what was going on, I delegated responsibilities because I had no choice. The team's response and overwhelming support reaffirmed to me that Unity had truly incredible people. The organization didn't miss a beat when I was away, which also showed me that the team was more than capable of rising to the challenge without me. Once I started feeling a bit better, I continued to empower, motivate, and challenge the team, but also continued to get out of their way. I was forced to focus on my core job and only the most important tasks as it was all I had the energy and ability to do.

I assessed our meetings and cancelled any from my schedule that did not directly serve our purpose. I told others to continue to attend meetings that were in their area of responsibility and gave the team and managers space to make their own decisions without needing my approval. I cut my meetings down from ten a day to two a day. I opted for a fifteen-minute phone call instead of an hour-long face-to-face meeting. I focused on what I like doing and what I do best, as well as what I felt the organization needed most. I needed to find better ways to take care of myself so I could take care of others and the organization. I had to focus and delegate. I also looked into any mental health supports I could find from an organizational perspective.

I added mental health benefits to our staff benefits plans immediately. I also applied to get donated licences to a meditation smartphone app called Headspace. I emailed the Headspace team, sharing my story of battling anxiety in a leadership role, and asked them for free licences to their software for our staff, artists, and youth in our programs. One week later, I got an email from Headspace that they wanted to donate 250 free Headspace meditation licences to us.

We were embodying self-care in our culture. We developed this new muscle as an organization by sharing vulnerabilities. Truly taking care of our people took care of productivity and built an authentic caring culture.

During this healing process, my wife, Mel, was my rock. She is so patient with me and caring. Also, our puppy, Olive, grounded me immediately in the present moment. Olive is a fluffy and sassy mini golden doodle with tons of loving energy, a cute, curly brown coat, and white spots on her paws and chest. She leaps at me with unconditional love, cuddles, and kisses when I come through the front door. My worries about past and future melt away in an instant every time I am with Olive. Seeing her boldly jump towards new people and experiences reminds me not to hide behind my fear.

Mel and Olive bring me heartfelt joy and help me cope with my anxiety and face my fears. Although I still have panic attacks, lose several nights of sleep, and am living with anxiety, I move forward. Panic comes up at the most random moments, like the time I went on the Harry Potter ride at Universal Studios and had one of the worst panic attacks I've ever experienced. It sounds silly even writing about it, but at least I can laugh about it today. It started when the large padded mechanism came down on my shoulders and chest securing my body in place. It clicked and locked. I felt trapped. My heart pumped and I began crying. This propelled me into panic as the ride began moving and I wanted off. When I got off the ride, I couldn't stop crying and shaking. The physical symptoms of anxiety rose up and shook in my chest and throat for days following. I had to learn to manage these intense episodes.

For me, being present is my new mission and a constant challenge. I am on a mission not to live in past or future but breathe the air right in front of me, right now. Experiencing and feeling what I feel as I'm feeling it, whether that is pleasant, unpleasant, or anything in between. Letting go of judgment, trying not to add judgment to what is. Even embracing the feeling of anxiety when it's pumping through my body, although not enjoyable, accepting it as it is. Not trying to resist the bad or chase the good. Even though it may sound corny, meditation and mindfulness have pushed me to become a better person in all aspects of my life. My mind might wander far off into the abyss, but I remind myself that my life is best lived here in the present. This is constant hard work for me, but the intention behind it changes my life every moment I catch myself getting lost in the vortex of spinning thoughts. I am learning to live with a new reality.

FINDING MY OUTLET AND COMMUNITY

Dance became my outlet for stress, anger, and pent-up emotions I hadn't dealt with. This art form and expression truly saved my life. Breakin' has been an outlet for so many social ills since its inception in the South Bronx in the 1970s. Because of its perfect blend of musicality, physicality, and storytelling with your body, it goes far beyond anything that can be said with words. Who would have thought a white Jewish kid would use it to help him work on his mental health? Yet here we are. Finding my outlet helped me find my voice.

This dance style is built on competition: the battle. It's interesting because as I went to therapy I began to learn that my anxiety could also be viewed as a battle. When I enter a battle in breakin', I size up the competition and respond to what people are doing, but most importantly I focus on myself and am present in the moment to respond to the music. When I went to therapy, my therapist challenged me to look at anxiety as though it was a battle, a challenge. This made it easier to face because I knew what it felt like to step to a really tough competitor, someone I thought was more skilled than I am. I just stepped into the cypher, I showed up, I was present, and I faced them. This is exactly what I began to do with my anxiety, face it. When the time to battle comes, stand up and face fear head on.

Being part of my crew built a sense of community when I needed it most. My crew was like a second family to me. When my parents were not well or things were too stressful at home, I would go to session and practise. They taught me how to dress, how to act, how to walk, how to be. We had each other's backs. This is a vital parallel — we need to have each other's backs in organizations and stand up for those who need support the most. We put people before profits and people before impact. We need to act like a crew to create a long-term responsible impact and build a caring culture.

Journal Entry — September 2, 2017
Biting my tongue

I'm in front of the people I care about the most. I'm here but I'm gone. They have no idea and I feel like I want to scream it out. Although not telling them is best for the organization, it's killing me inside. How do I hold this?

Every conversation I have another conversation in my head. Should I tell them? Should I wait?

I've agreed with my board chair, Adam, that I will wait to tell everyone at the same time.

Holding this secret is like holding an elephant back from a peanut. Do elephants eat peanuts? Maybe a monkey to a banana. Either way, this is freaking intense.

I bite my tongue, I carry on in silence.

Facing my anxiety meant I started to take better care of myself, which sparked new forms of self-reflection. I realized that I was living in my comfort zone. I was not adding new value to Unity. I wasn't learning new things. I was coasting. I really had given the organization and the team all that I could give. Things became predictable. Just because it is easy, does not mean it is right. As my Grampa always said, "The easy way is the wrong way, and the hard way is the right way." I was only thirty-one, Unity was my only long-term job, so I didn't even know what I was fully capable of. It felt like it was time to leave, but I felt stuck. Maybe I just needed a sabbatical.

The process was extremely painful, but I leaned into the discomfort and began to trust that the universe would hold me. I struggled with a lack of control of what the future might hold for me. Just because I felt finished didn't mean Unity was.

Journal Entry — January 4, 2018

It was time for me to spread my wings.
To let Unity grow up.
To do my next big thing.
To trust all of the amazing people who helped raise my
    only child. And to let go.
Time to trust that I've done the most I can do.
It's not about me.
It's about the work.
About our cause.
The legacy will continue on in new and profound ways
    without me at the table or even in the kitchen.

I will cheer the team on from afar with a proud grin on
    my face.
To celebrate their success.
To let the team, fail, fall, and learn on their own.
To trust in new leadership, to support new ways forward.
It's time to move on.
To step back so someone else can truly step forward.
To let go.

The question became, do I have the courage to really ride out the awkwardness and fear and build the job I want? Or will I just do what I know how to do because that is what people do? I do what I'm good at. I do what I've done my whole life. Why would I do anything else? Because I am not my past. Do I conform to expectation? Or do I break loose and follow the moment? Crash and create, using the energy that this major life transition creates to learn, grow, and move on. So why does my conscious thought only dream up things I can do that I am familiar with? Because I like being comfortable. I feel like learning for me really stopped when I became comfortable at Unity. It's time to leave that behind.

I'm so used to having something to do. Something that I can apply my skills to, something with a meaningful contribution. When I left Unity on March 1, 2018, I didn't have a plan or a job or a career path. I was worried that my abilities to do work and feel productive would diminish and fizzle. I hoped my fear about this would be the very thing that prevents my fire from burning out. The desire, hope, and momentum of the free fall.

"EVEN WHEN IT'S TIME TO GO, IT FEELS IMPOSSIBLE TO LEAVE."[3]

Succession is a lonely topic. When I made the decision to leave, I felt like I couldn't talk to *anyone* about succession, because all the people I trusted the most were key stakeholders in Unity and I didn't want to instill doubt. But we needed to have real conversations about succession so that the organization understood all the challenges that come along with it. I didn't know where to start, and it felt scary to talk about.

Stepping down was the most difficult but most important decision I ever made in my working career. I thought this would be my job for life. Since I founded Unity, it had grown from a volunteer group in my basement to an organization that has impacted the lives of over a quarter of a million young people with fifteen staff and over eighty paid artist educators in the hip hop community. Not only were we having significant impact, but we were providing dream jobs with strong team culture.

Unity married all my passions in life: hip hop (as a b-boy), mental health (from personal experiences in my life), and community development. I literally created my dream job. Why would I *ever* leave something so perfect? Sometimes founders of organizations leave when things aren't going well. I decided to do the complete opposite. Unity had never been stronger than it was at the time I left. Our impact was growing; our staff, board of directors, and volunteers were rock solid; our partnerships were deep and diversified; our artists were superheroes; our evaluations were robust; and our funders were engaged. If there ever was a good time for me to move on and plant my feet somewhere else, it was now. We had a clear co-created vision, strategy, and theory of change as the organization's foundation and compass moving forward.

---

3   Quoted from Rebecca Fishman Lipsey, Radical Partners

My departure created space for a new leader to steer this ship in the direction that the community commanded.

I realized at this time that what it took to build Unity from the ground up is not what the organization needed to sustain it. Unity could live on without me; I just had to build up the courage to actually make the decision to leave. This organization could continue without me, and I could contribute to new spaces. I see succession as an opportunity to amplify the impact I can create in my lifetime, by giving others real opportunity. I walked away with no board seat, no staff role, no involvement. It was a clean break. My final message to the team was, "You are in charge."

There are many conflicting feelings and priorities when leaving an organization you are part of creating. Nothing lasts forever, but unfortunately some great organizations fall apart due to founders or longstanding leaders who cannot let go of their baby. This happens too often in the non-profit sector, and there are many reasons why. Sometimes people care so much about something that they hurt the very thing they are trying to protect. I felt this myself, but pushed to do the right thing and not get in the way during the transition. Also, because I had sacrificed so much as a founder to build this organization, sometimes I felt like someone owed me something at the end of such a long term. I hate to even admit this feeling, but it was very real for me. It was a key moment; I had to directly confront and challenge my ego. Self-awareness and deep reflection saved me from hurting the organization I spent most of my life building and caring for.

I did everything in my being to set up Unity for success. I organized and shared everything I could think of, including key documents, knowledge, resources, history, contacts, and relationships. I gave as openly as I could, and I fully trusted in the incredibly strong successor, Rebecca Harrison, and the team.

If Unity had been a business, and not a charity, I would have been able to sell the organization. That isn't how it works in the non-profit sector. We just walk away, even though it takes the same effort to build a non-profit from scratch — if not more, considering work is done on minimal budgets and with public scrutiny on where funds are spent. There was ultimately nothing tangible to support my next step in life. Even though I paid myself fairly towards my last few years at Unity, if you average my salary over the fifteen years I dedicated to the organization, it worked out to less than minimum wage.

I can see why founders get wound up in the ego around this. This reflection helped me understand why some founders feel conflicted when leaving due to a harmful overemphasis on their own sacrifice. I really did not do it for the money, and in essence I decided what to pay myself in the early days. I can see what drives founders leaving their organizations to seek pity in their sacrifice. The old "I've given up so much to make this possible" song and dance. Even though sometimes I felt this way, I wanted to set a different example and not buy into that shitty story. I did everything I could to not transition from a place of self-defense but from a place of trust and deep pride for the team's contributions.

I also knew I would miss the energy of working with such amazing people. I got to work with some of my favourite people in the entire world. I just had to build up the courage to actually make the decision to leave and believe that I could create something new again from scratch. We empowered a great team and had a highly capable new executive director that I felt confident could take the organization to the next level of growth and success without me. I knew that I had so much to give to improve the effectiveness of non-profits in our country and all over the world. It is in my DNA to keep going. But at Unity, I knew my time was coming to an end.

Flipping Succession: Model Healthy Relationships

I remember in my last year at Unity before choosing to move on, it was day one of the Unity Festival, our biggest event of the year. This year's festival landed on the same day a game was released: Pokémon GO, an augmented reality video game you can play on your smartphone. Some days I played Pokémon for five hours carrying around battery packs with me to charge my phone; it became another escape. I remember walking away from the team setting up the festival for over an hour to play this game and catch new Pokémon. As I was walking, I bumped into the festival coordinator, Andrew "Andy Capp" Hicks, in an alleyway behind the venue, and he asked me what I was doing. I shamefully told him I was catching a Pokémon. It sounds ridiculous, but this was the first moment I knew my heart was no longer in it.

There are several things I had to come to terms with throughout this process. First and most important, it's not about me, it is about the cause and the impact that Unity was having in empowering youth through hip hop. While this may seem obvious, I have seen so many leaders who don't know when to step back and let others step forward. They stay in their role out of fear. Fear of loss, fear of never doing anything as great again, fear of financial stability, fear of their organization failing without them.

I realized that when I trusted the right people with a responsibility, they almost always rose to the occasion. Giving people trust, encouragement, and credit for their work has proven to uncover some of Unity's best leaders and natural successors. Equally as important, I was incredibly thankful that the board and succession committee selected Rebecca Harrison, who did an extraordinary job of continuing to grow Unity with the team after I left.

I had to accept that my baby had grown up — and so had I. I wanted and needed a different experience if I was to keep growing — and so did Unity. I needed to let it go so it could spread its wings and fly without me.

It is not my intention to oversimplify the complexities of succession. If you haven't experienced succession personally, especially as a founder, please be mindful of how you bring it up. Talking about succession is vital. Poor succession, however, is often the demise of many great charities and businesses.

Succession is completely different depending on our unique context and circumstances. It is easier said than done, so please be patient, understanding, and empathetic, and learn from other people's mistakes. If you ever want to talk about succession, I'm always down to chat. I think we need to talk more openly about succession and share our stories of success to inspire other leaders to let go and build successful futures for themselves. We need to start an honest and open intergenerational conversation for better succession.

Succession is difficult because there are so many opposing dynamics that no one can see. For example, to do this well, I had to respect the board and search committee process while voicing my feelings on what I felt Unity needed. This was a difficult tango, but

I learned quickly. At the same time, I didn't want to cast a big and ugly founder shadow over the next executive director.

For me, the best way to do this was to not stick around. I made the decision to not be on the board of directors because I felt it could possibly send the wrong message to Rebecca. I wholeheartedly trusted her leadership. Succession is about genuinely modelling healthy relationships, trusting that the organization could fly without me, and truly letting go. It's also about selecting a strong successor and having a committed team to support the work that's needed to enable the organization to continue blooming, growing, and evolving.

In effect, I honoured a non-compete clause that I had never signed. I passed on all of my relationships and contacts to the Unity team, even though I didn't have to. I did this because I knew it would help Unity succeed.

"TO STEP TOWARD YOUR DESTINY, YOU HAVE TO STEP AWAY FROM YOUR SECURITY."[4]

As I transitioned out of my role, I learned that this was not going to be as easy as I had thought. How do I do what's right for the organization in the long run while still taking care of myself in the process? I wanted to make sure that Unity's needs were met, but I also had to think about my own. This included everything from my personal finances, career options, and mental health to the organization's finances, strategy, management, and systems.

---

4   Attributed to Craig Groeschel

I learned a lot from my mentors and peers in the non-profit sector who founded and ran their organizations for many years. After watching several peers propel their organizations into crisis upon their departure, I learned most founders and long-time leaders have a terribly difficult time letting go. Often these situations ended with founders getting voted out of their own organization by their board or, worse, hanging on so tightly that they killed their organization with ego. This is no joke. I didn't want to be *that* person.

At the same time, I can understand why this happens so often. I felt the conflicting internal and external motivations that could lead someone down this path of hurting the very thing they care so much about. It is a complex internal battle and was difficult for me to understand and articulate. So, I did everything I could to prevent this and constantly checked in with my conflicting internal dialogue. I had to fight my childish thoughts constantly throughout this process:

Why would I help transfer my knowledge as I leave?

Why would I give up all the contacts and relationships I've built in my life?

Why would I spend extra time building systems and transferring relationships?

I felt like I had already sacrificed so much, but I had to confront my ego and defensive reactions. I did what I believed was best for Unity, the team, the new executive director, and ultimately the youth. Then Rebecca and the team picked up the torch. As a result of this reflection and working with many founders and long-time leaders who were leaving their organizations, I began to share this framework as "steps to transitions" with anyone I knew who was considering making one:

I had to resist the temptation to fall into a selfish and self-destructive line of thinking. Although I will tell you, it was vivid. Sometimes this defensive self-sabotage was so strong I needed to go home and meditate. I knew my big goal was to have Unity succeed without me, and I needed

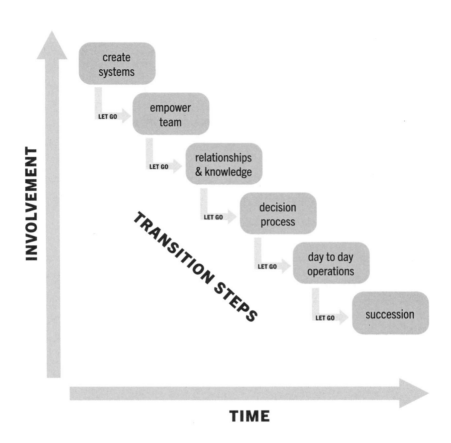

to focus on doing the right thing to get there so I could fully let go. The date was set for March 1, 2018.

I wanted to be involved in choosing my successor, but I realized it was best for Unity if the board of directors and succession committee did that work. I gave feedback on what my job entailed to the recruiter to help form the job description, organized files to transfer knowledge, transferred key contacts, created a healthy funding reserve, and supported onboarding in any way I could. My goal was to create a runway for the new leader, but not get in the way of hiring. The board and succession committee hired a recruiter to screen candidates and facilitated the hiring process. The committee even included former Unity staff. This way they would be fully accountable and empowered behind the vision of the leader they choose.

I wanted to stay involved with the organization immediately after the succession, but I didn't want to cast a shadow over the new leader's vision or disempower them in any decision-making. I wanted to know what was going on, but I didn't want people to keep coming to me for answers. I wanted to support the new executive director in the transition, but I didn't want to overstep, making them feel like they need my approval to make change.

I was conflicted: I wanted to rip off the Band-Aid and leave as soon as possible, but I wanted to provide the team and new leader with everything they needed to succeed without me, which takes time. I felt really terrible inside letting go of my baby, but at the same time I wanted to instill complete confidence in the new leader. I was so thankful to have a strong incoming executive director, who put in so much work into making the transition successful.

I didn't consider my own personal needs enough in the process around identity, feeling productive, and the grief that I would feel. The big thing I wrestled with on a daily basis throughout the transition was, "How do I show up to the office with confidence in the process while I feel like I am dying inside?" Even though I was confident this was the right decision, I was grieving. This triggered strong and intense anxiety.

I was losing a piece of myself. However, I cared so much about the success of the transition that I had to develop coping mechanisms so that I didn't show my inner conflict. I really did trust my team, Rebecca, and the plan we had, but sometimes my natural instinct was clouded with emotion. I was going through an identity crisis that was ego-stripping, yet necessary.

I remember attending my final fundraiser which was framed as my "last party" with Unity. We raised over two hundred thousand dollars from this event, and for the first time introduced Rebecca Harrison, the new executive director, to all of our supporters. Rebecca and the team worked hard to make this a dream transition. Rebecca jumped with both feet right into the deep end and thrived. The room was packed with a decade of past and current supporters, artists, staff, alumni, funders, board members, community members, and teachers, and really anyone who cared deeply about Unity. Everyone I cared about was under one roof. It was like nothing I had ever experienced before. The room was filled with tears of joy, pride, unforgettable memories, and accomplishment. I cried a ton that night. It was overwhelming, and for me, it was closure. The only way I can describe it to people was that it felt like I attended my own funeral. This was a big moment for me in letting go and passing the torch.

My board chair, Adam, was a model example of how to do what's best for the organization and for me as a person. He led an effective succession process with the support of the board and a fantastic non-profit recruiter, Suzanne Clark. Adam really looked out for me over the years while maintaining the appropriate advisory and governance role of the board. This is such a fine balance. He is a down-to-earth mentor and a fantastic boss. Below is an email he sent me right after I broke the news to him on September 7, 2017:

Hey Mikey,

I just wanted to respond and say you and Unity are going to be ok through this. We are going to make mistakes and there will be bumps in the road, but you have a long and bright future as does Unity.

All the best,
— Adam

Acknowledging and celebrating what we had done was a vital step in beginning to truly let go. I received many beautiful and kind messages from our team in my last few days at Unity that still bring me to tears. Below are just a few of those beautiful messages that I took with me as inspiration and held close to my heart as I stepped out of comfort and into the unknown:

Mikey,

Thank you for always making time to listen

Thank you for agreeing to mentor and learn with me when I took on the initiative lead role, sharing useful guidance and modelling not-for-profit management

Thank you for putting artists before the art

Thank you for valuing my mental and physical health

Thank you for always being so awkward

Thank you for staying humble even though we all know that you are actually really intelligent and have a special expertise

Thank you for pushing me . . . even it if dislocated my shoulder that one time

Thank you for your vulnerability within your position of power

Thank you for deciding to take risks and prioritize yourself and your health and future

Thank you for taking young people seriously

Thank you for taking yourself, your ideas, and your art and your dreams seriously

Thank you for working hard to create and ensure there are safe spaces for young people to express themselves and build through hip hop cultures

Mikey, you are about to embark on a new, exciting journey. I'm so excited for you. Have the best, most silly, challenging, and rewarding travel experience! Do whatever the fuck you want. Make stupid decisions. Stay up all night and see a sunrise. Play!! Meet new people. Be alone. Breathe. Love, just BE. We will all be here waiting for your return, doing our own thing and rockin' it with Unity. OMG you're getting married soon-ish too! Awwww so many things to celebrate. Love you so much. Mikey, please stay in touch and let's go to a playground or climb a tree soon.

— Redge, in a letter on my final day at Unity, March 1, 2018

Hey Mikey! I just wanted to take the chance and say thank YOU from every molecule of my being! If it wasn't for UNITY and the People involved I'm not sure where I would be, however, I can confidently say UNITY has been a very huge factor in changing my life. When I came here as a newcomer, the first 3 years that I was here, I had no social & support circle thus leading to some mental health quirks. Also, my dance was dying 'cause I knew of no place that could accommodate me. Nevertheless, I found the hip hop drop-in program at Rightfoot led by Catherine and that would change the direction of my life forever. I started to be more involved, built a strong and needed circle, overall giving me a sense of purpose. Then being able to participate and doing work for Unity really humbled me as a being and put everything into perspective. Personally, the emphasis on community made me realize how vital it is, especially in a fast-paced city like Toronto, that we need to look out for each other.

Can't be more grateful to what you've brought into being, Mikey!

I will be forever thankful and continue push forward in the spirit of UNITY.

Many blessings and much love.

— Rainer

On the first day I moved to Toronto. The first evening, I was so anxious. I was with friends in a park and was hiding my tears. I had no idea what my life would become. In that friend circle someone was a staff at Unity and I remember the whole scene, I remember the sound coming out of my mouth saying "*I* want to work for Unity." I will forever remember my journey all the way to contacting you, getting ready to meet, our meeting, and the energy that was exchanged to how "full" and how of a giant I felt when I walked out of that coffee shop.

Thank you for taking a chance on me and changing my life. Thank you for your integrity, your sincerity, and vulnerability when you told me "I don't know why, but I trust you." These words are to me a sign that we were meant to meet that we are part of a mission that is greater than who we are and at that moment it could be felt.

Since then I am forever grateful for all the times I didn't have to hide my tears or my passion around you. You have made me feel loved for who I am and that is the most beautiful gift you could ever offer.

Thank you for having faith that my challenges are my strengths. You have made me feel proud of myself, and Unity has made me do and accomplish things I could never believe I would be capable of. The chance you took on me and your faith is what I want to be able to bring in my work, and I hope with all my heart that at a turning point in your life someone will offer you that. You deserve all of the chances.

The first day of the festival, I gave myself the courage to drive the truck by holding onto the quote, "A ship is safe in the harbour, but that's not what ships are built for." I told myself "time to sail." It's your time to sail. To pick up your anchor and go on a journey.

I have so much Respect, Love, and Excitement for you, Mikey.

You are your most greatest creation. Thank you for being a true role model. For taking care of others like no one else but taking care of yourself and your inner child, your intuition, your own inner plant that needed to grow, for taking care of the mover that you are and making moves, creating flow in your life, and for reminding me to always take care of myself.

You already know this, but you mean so much to me. You are not only a mentor but a real friend and definitely like a real brother to me. Thank you for being in my life.

Open your wings, open your eyes and your heart, feel the earth between your toes, and sing at the top of your lungs. You have me as a friend forever to be ninjas with and sit under trees (and dance).

I wish you an amazing trip. This is the spring of your life. I wish you emotional, spiritual, and artistic blooms. Gosh, have so much fun. Say hi to the clouds, the kangaroos, and Tafiya for me ☺

Love Love Love Love
!! Mikey Mikey Mikey Mikey !!
There is no buddy like you.
Cat XO<3

Cactuses are spiky and rough; foreboding and strange; but most of all they remind us of nature's irreverent brutality and inexplicability. But many people never consider a cactus's origins and often the magnificent landscapes and ecosystems are forgotten — but not this time.

You created a beautiful ecosystem. You thrived in your ecosystem. You formed symbiotic relationships with other fellow plants and created microcosms for others to thrive within the ecosystem.

Anyhow, every plant must evolve. As you venture into new and unfamiliar systems, learn new skills, and expand your mind . . . remember that a cactus is one of the most resilient plants on Earth. Your potential is limitless. Never doubt your worth, ability, or energy. There's always room in a cactus's tank!

Enjoy your travels, Mikey! much love ☺

— Mahad

1. How do you know when is the right time for you to leave your organization?
2. What do you need in the next phase of your career (finances, lifestyle, learning, challenge, etc.)?
3. What does your organization need in its next evolution (team, funds, board, strategy, etc.)?
4. What overlaps do you notice in your needs and your organization's needs?
5. What differences do you notice?
6. What would a completely successful transition out of your organization look like?
7. What steps would you need to take to ensure you get there?
8. What tangible steps can you take today to plan your future succession? (Keep in mind, everyone eventually leaves.)
9. What can you do to set up your organization for success after you leave? (Consider how letting go plays a role in your organization's future success.)
10. Do you plan to be involved with the organization after you leave? If so, how do you hope to be involved?
11. How can you ensure you do not get in the way of the organization's future evolution?
12. What alternative options might you consider exploring as your organization evolves? (For example: bring in new leadership, merge with similar organization(s), close down if your mission is no longer being served, revise mission/strategy based on evolving need in your community, etc.)

RE-IGNITE
Launching Epic

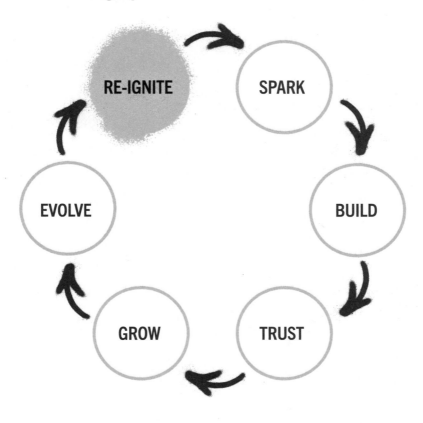

Hands down, March of 2018 was one of the toughest months of my life. It was like being stripped of my identity. Although I made the decision for the right reasons, in the right way, it still hurt. After leaving Unity on March 1, after fifteen years, I boarded a plane the next day to San Francisco, where I would connect with a flight to New Zealand. But something wasn't right. In the weeks leading up to my flight, I couldn't sleep. When I boarded the plane in Toronto, I had an anxiety attack. While waiting to board the connecting flight in San Francisco, I decided I just couldn't do it. I asked the airport staff at the flight check-in counter to remove my bags from the plane. My body was literally shaking.

Prior to all of this, I had been meeting with an amazing therapist for over a year. His name was Dr. Joseph Regan, and he helped me through some of my darkest days. He was an incredible man and truly saved my life. To my deep shock and sadness, on February 9, 2018, he passed away, only a few days before my last day at Unity. It all of a sudden felt like everything in my life was falling apart.

After missing my flight, I couldn't pick myself up. I felt deeply embarrassed, ashamed, and like I'd hit rock bottom. After a week of dark depression and feeling hopeless in San Francisco, I needed to do something. So, I rented a car and drove around to see cool shit. I saw the biggest tree in the world, "General Sherman," some kickass Yosemite Mountains, and coastal San Diego beauty. Then I decided to give surprise visits to my dad and Grampa in Tennessee and Florida. I needed to be around people I loved.

I just began to follow what felt right, day by day, which was something I've never done before in my life. I always had a path, a direction, a purpose. Anxiety and depression are no joke. I've never felt as depressed in my life as I had when I missed that flight. It was scary. I felt a lot of guilt and shame, but I realized I needed to be kinder to myself. Travelling solo while fighting this stuff is even more confusing and challenging. I was completely alone with my negative spinning thoughts, feeling a lack of self-worth. Writing this book became my therapy. It became the only thing making me excited to get up in the morning.

BACK TO BUILD: MY NEXT PLANE

Date: October 12, 2017

Bro, heard on the street first, then read on fb, now this . . . add me to the mighty chorus of people who appreciate SO MUCH all your work; who understand the healing through the nation you have spread; you, who fought for a stage then shared it then built steps to it then built many more stages across this country; you, who put CHEQUES in people's pockets for doing what they love! (true say word on the street is UNITY Always pays, and on time, you're like the fucking Lannisters of the community arts movement minus the well, you know . . .) Anyway I know as much as anyone it took a community for it all to happen . . . but there is such a thing as a catalyst :)

Big up to you and your inspiration/desperation/perspiration.

Not in a rush to see what's next.

I know it will be real

— Julian Diego [community partner/arts advocate/friend]

About six months post-Unity, I began to resurface from my grief. It was much more difficult than I had expected. The feelings of missing the team and losing a part of myself lingered in me for months — and still do to this day. I care so much about Unity, but it's best for me to let it grow up without me. It was the best transition I could have hoped for. I am so thankful that Rebecca Harrison took over after me. She has created space for the impact to continue to thrive. She is a truly gifted leader; I have a lot to learn from her approach. I have spoken mostly about my transition process so far, but the succession could not have been as effective and smooth without Rebecca's vital contribution holding the ship together, continuing to empower the team, and moving things forward. Now I needed to define my next steps in life.

I began to feel like myself again. The biggest gap was not feeling productive. It's weird to have a huge number of people depend on you at work and then wake up to be accountable only to myself. It felt good, but also made me feel worthless. I soon began to define my value through rebuilding friendships, seeing family, getting married to the girl of my dreams, Mel, and getting a mini golden doodle puppy named Olive. My life was no longer defined by work, and it felt super weird. There were some ideas I had in me that I could not nurture while I was at Unity. Now I had the space to plant new seeds for future growth.

Waking up, going to coffee shops, not sure what I was working on or why and what it was ultimately contributing to — it felt very raw, like the start of Unity and learning to break all over again. Paralyzed by choice and a lack of choice at the same time, I decided to make a list of things that bothered me about our world that I felt I could impact. This list grew and grew into over twenty-five pages of ideas. I began to break down these ideas and chip away at anything I could. I was building the plane while flying it again, throwing myself into the deep end, starting with issues that were close to my heart and part of my story. I began searching for my next "spark."

I decided on June 24, 2018, to register a federal corporation, which I decided would be a social enterprise called EPIC Leadership with a focus on empowering social impact leaders to grow and thrive. EPIC stands for Excellent People Impacting Communities. I had a direction again, but no plan. EPIC would be my new compass.

With a brand-new social enterprise, I was back to square one, but the difference this time was I could tap into a network I had built over fifteen years. For some things, I had to go back to learning from ground zero. It was a painful, ego-challenging experience to realize I was now a one-person team again with nothing except a lot of drive and puppy love as fuel.

My network was quick to take meetings with me as people were interested to see what my next move might be. The expectations others had of me of doing something "big" or "great" in my next chapter were challenging. I realized that I cared more about what other people thought about me than I wanted to. I wanted to define my own path and remove these unhealthy outside pressures. But my internal voice kept calling me to do something big again. I wanted to leverage the experiences I had to make a big, positive, and responsible change. To start something new and impact specific issues based on my experience.

The next chapter began with a logo drawn on a napkin, a long list of ideas, and a list of all the people I had met over the years who I wanted to grab coffee with. Every day I woke up unsure what I was doing, but driven by an underlying force to leave the world in a better place than I found it. Some of the areas I care deeply about include mental health in the workplace, succession planning, peer support in the non-profit sector, and how to build a grassroots organization from the ground up. So I went back to building, starting each morning with hot coffee and an open mind, driven by passion for addressing injustices that underlie the non-profit sector. Eventually I hired Diamond Osoteo from Unity to help me build a new website, as well as Caerina Abrenica (a Unity youth alumni who now runs several Unity programs), and Mike "Fate" Brobbey (a Unity artist educator) to design a logo for EPIC. Caerina also designed the b-boy and b-girl characters you see throughout this book and on its cover.

It's been a rollercoaster over the past year building EPIC. Sometimes I would leave meetings with people and walk away not clear why I had even set them, only to find later that those meetings were planting seeds for future opportunities. I got to collaborate on the issues I cared about. I needed to trust in the process. I forgot what it is like to lay the foundation for a new project. It is humbling to be back to square one. Back to build. It's challenging me at my core, and I'm fuelled by learning each day.

I was back to the hustle again, building the plane while flying it. Except this time, I had done a lot of deep reflection on how I hoped to build towards my next impact. I wanted to tackle social issues at their root cause, finding leverage points earlier in the cycle to have greater impact, and be more responsible at every step. Ultimately, leverage points are areas you can invest in and improve to deliver exponential impact. It is focusing on the right areas, at the right times, with the right approach, with the right people at the table, to create deeper, wider, and more sustained impact on social issues. In an organization this could look like building stronger team culture so there is less staff turnover, thereby delivering improved interactions with clients. It could also look like more clearly telling an organization's impact story to funders so they can raise more funds to sustain a needed service.

That realization led me to reflect on these questions:

- How can I support leaders running high-impact initiatives on their journey?
- How can I advocate to grow the pie of funding available in government, business, and philanthropy?
- How can I encourage flow of resources to high-impact organizations that are not receiving adequate support?
- How do I save time, money, and energy for organizations so they can focus on their mission?
- How can I support the well-being of leaders so they can better support their mission and their teams?
- How can I support the next generation of emerging leaders to grow and thrive?

I wrote the questions down in a list, and I began taking small steps in testing the answers to them. I am more confident in facing disagreements head-on. I focus on value alignment with all partners, and I experiment with small ideas with community involvement to test my assumptions. Everything seems to be moving faster than when I first started Unity. I'm beginning to discover how to have an impact at a systemic level. I'm working with municipalities, funders, boards, executive directors, and frontline staff as catalysts for greater impact. I know I'm on the right track because I feel uncomfortable; I'm excited to wake up, and I'm learning new things daily. Here we go, again.

DISCOVERING IMPACT: A CONTINUOUS LEARNING CYCLE

We built Unity by learning from previous experiences while challenging ourselves to never stop learning. In order to sustain our impact, we continually questioned our assumptions and adapted. We were always discovering, reflecting, and reinventing. This is how I'm now building EPIC. I aim to lead with humility, honesty, and vulnerability. My progress isn't linear, but a reminder that learning is cyclical. I try to remain a student to create the most responsible impact possible. It's a constant discovery. When I feel I know something too well, I often get overly comfortable. When I sense too much comfort, I try to put myself in new situations and learn something new from the ground up. This re-invention re-ignites my spark. The complacency of comfort kills my drive and effectiveness.

BREAKING THE CYCLE 15

I feel proud of where I landed. I feel proud of leaving Unity strong and purposeful. This transition took a lot out of me emotionally and physically, but I am stronger for it.

In 2019, I scrolled through Facebook events and came across Breaking the Cycle 15. This is an event I started with a team of volunteers fifteen years ago. It was taken over by Unity's university chapters, made up of program alumni who had now grown up and gone on to attend various universities. These youth created Unity student clubs at their schools to build on the values and vibe Unity had sparked for them.

I felt a deep pride to watch the Breaking the Cycle event being run after fifteen years, without me involved in any way. In fact, I wasn't even invited to it! I was randomly scrolling through Facebook events and stumbled upon it. I decided to attend and see how it had evolved. I was so proud. I remember glowing from the side of the room with a huge smile. The venue was packed with new and familiar faces. Youth I met in their high school almost ten years ago were running the show. I cheered them on. Unity was now owned by the community. It was out of my hands, and I couldn't be prouder.

ADVOCACY FOR GRASSROOTS ORGANIZATIONS

Almost a year after leaving Unity, I worked with the City of Toronto to write a report on the need for a stabilization-funding program for grassroots arts agencies with several partners. I wanted to be a part of advocating beyond a single organization. It was a proposal we had been pitching with a few grassroots organizations before I left Unity to advocate for ongoing government support as a collective. I wrote a report outlining the need for government resources to sustain six grassroots arts organizations that developed significant artistic talent in our city and had contributed over a decade of impact but were struggling to survive. In 2019, I was thrilled to see nine hundred thousand dollars get approved in the city budget as a result of this advocacy. This was in a year where there were tons of cuts elsewhere, so it was a big win. I was looking for avenues to support impact on a systems level. Again, I reaffirmed for myself that I'm on the right track.

THE POWER OF PEER SUPPORT

After attending several leadership development programs over the years, I always dreamed of running a leadership program that had no agenda. No lead facilitators. Just leaders gathered together in a safe place where they can speak openly about personal and organizational challenges, work through those challenges, provide support to one another, and hold one another accountable for change. I believe that dedicated peer groups could harness expertise of diverse social impact leaders in different stages of their career, with different organization sizes and across multiple sub-sectors. There must be a way to create a space where these leaders can learn from each other. Something with no curriculum but with a process to facilitate peer learning, sharing, and support.

Every time I thought about this concept or explained it to someone, I got more excited about it. I knew I needed to do something about it. It was my new spark based on my recent experiences running Unity. After burning out and triggering a mental health condition, I felt this deep desire to support the remarkable people who run social purpose organizations so they could sustain their impact in healthier ways.

I had to test this idea out and see if it was really as worthwhile as I believed. In 2019, I woke up one morning, built a website in less than forty-eight hours, and launched EPIC xChange, a peer support program to facilitate sharing and working through personal and organizational challenges among senior non-profit leaders. Within two weeks we had twenty people signed up. I went back to building based on a personal spark, and I was able to leverage my networks and strengths to get it off the ground and give it a shot.

Since launching, the experience has been transformational beyond my expectations. I believe people who run organizations have profound genius and need peers to exchange with to get through difficult times, stop to celebrate success, and take care of themselves. We are just beginning, but I know we are onto something. I am back to building, and it feels great. I am fuelled by learning and discovering how this program can be better. EPIC xChange is the plane that wakes me up every day, so I can build it while flying.

JOURNEY > DESTINATION

After spending some time travelling, I turned to writing this book and figuring out where I wanted to spend my time for the foreseeable future. I'm on that search every day. With my book written and a year of learning under my belt, I am excited to see what lies ahead. There is no rush. I ground myself and keep my eyes open in the present moment.

Thankfully, I've become more patient, more kind to myself, and happier to only work on the things that are satisfying my true goals.

I told myself I want to do five things in my new phase of life:

1. Work with awesome people (no harmful egos)
2. Make a positive and responsible contribution in the world
3. Don't hurt myself to help others
4. Focus on friends, family, and dogs
5. Have fun!

Something I've only begun to digest is that life isn't linear and work isn't life. This has been an important year of experimentation, learning, and growth post-Unity. I have tried a lot of things that I felt were outside of my comfort zone: creating a solo dance production on struggling with mental illness in a leadership role; teaching a class at the University of Toronto on enhancing non-profit impact; facilitating full-day workshops for municipalities; writing a book; getting my coaching certification; joining the board of directors at JAYU, Big Brothers Big Sisters Toronto, and RISE Arts and Community Services; getting certified to implement mental health policies in companies; helping launch an innovative granting model with the Toronto Foundation to distribute nearly $1 million through oral presentations instead of written applications; and the list goes on. I'm back to building, and I need new skills to get there. I am always a student.

I have realized that I don't need to be an expert in any of these things to do them well. I find it rewarding to try things I'm super uncomfortable with and sometimes come out the other end with great feedback. Sometimes not. Every time I have fallen, though, I have jumped right back in with more experience.

I feel like I'm developing a dream team of people I love to work with, but I am not sure how we will all work together one day. I believe it's *all* about people. I want to continue supporting healthy transitions for long-term leaders; building capacity for high-potential, high-impact organizations; and exploring real pain points of real people on the ground trying to make a difference in the world.

To do this, or anything, I have had to learn to have more balance in my life. The anxiety is still there, but I am able to live with it. I am building EPIC at my own pace, in my own way. It's a work in progress, and I don't feel a sense of urgency to figure it out tomorrow. Organic growth feels like the right step. My vision is tangible and developing. I want to use all that I have learned to empower leaders and organizations that are looking to create a positive and respectful impact in the world. What's not clear is how that may manifest.

It's the journey that has led to my best success, learning, and relationships, not the destination. As best said by one of the youth participants and artist educators at Unity, JP Manabat: "It's not what I did, but what I was doing."

NOW IT'S YOUR TURN . . .

Build planes.
    Discover impact.
        Flip strengths.
            Trust crew.
                Show and prove.
                    Be kind to yourself.
                        Reflect and evolve.

Spark, Build, Trust, Grow, Evolve, Re-Ignite.
I wish you well on your journey in building and discovering impact.

TOOLS & RESOURCES

For more info on what EPIC is currently up to and how you can get involved go to epicleadership.ca.

Here are some resources you can access to dig deeper into building your responsible impact (epicleadership.ca/bookresources):

1. Finance Tools: budget, cash flow, audit, expense policy, reserve policy, delegation of authority, cheque request, expense reimbursement/petty cash sign out, internal process timeline
2. Board Tools: by-laws, skills matrix, role description, meeting agenda, onboarding package
3. Partnership Tools: partnership agreement, partner prospect list, partnership strategy framework
4. Program Tools: codes of conduct for working with youth, incident report, program flyers/program guide for schools

5. HR Tools: HR policy manual, compensation grid, employee performance review, grievance form, staff goals and objectives, job posting, onboarding checklist, organizational chart, artist contractor pricing chart, team values poster
6. Volunteer Tools: volunteer program outline, safety tips for volunteers, training agenda, volunteer recruitment flyer
7. Fundraising Tools: prospect list, revenue pipeline, pitch decks, holiday donation letter, in-kind donation letter, funder thank you art
8. Sponsorship Tools: sponsorship levels grid, sponsor tracking form, sponsorship opportunities form, sponsorship scenario planning
9. Evaluation Tools: process survey and example results, creative evaluation example, evaluation process timeline
10. Marketing Tools: annual report/case for support (longer version), case for support (shorter version), brand identity guidelines, branding strategy, social media guidelines, national TV commercial, press release
11. Risk Management Tools: organization risk management template, third party event policies, theory of change
12. Succession Tools: 100-day onboarding plan, succession planning committee timeline, announcement sample

TIMELINE

1992   My mom was diagnosed with schizophrenia

Mental health became a big part of my life

1999   My mom and dad divorced, and I moved back and forth between parents

My stress began to build

2000   I found breakin', and it became my outlet and community

I practised every day; it became my escape

2001   Battled to get into Maximum Efficiency Crew (MEC)

Became immersed in hip hop

MEC became a second family to me

2003	Ran first ever Hip Hop Away from Violence show as a grade 11 class project at my high school, Thornlea Secondary
	Proceeds were donated to the charity Leave Out ViolencE (LOVE)
2004	Joined the LOVE board of directors as a youth member to learn how to run a non-profit
	Hip Hop Away From Violence became a program at LOVE
	Became student council president and made Hip Hop Away from Violence our big event
	Began to build a movement of volunteers, artists, and community-engaged supporters
2005–2006	Attended York University and registered a student club called LOVE at York
	Ran a breakin' battle called Breaking the Cycle to raise money for our programs
	Grew programs from one to four high schools
	Held community vision meetings in my basement
	Got an office at York University
2007	LOVE asked me to register an independent organization
	Registered non-profit "UNITY Charity" and renamed club at York to UNITY at York

Won $5,000 pitch contest at Top 20 Under 20's conference, our first seed money

Unity became a program of the Phoenix Community Works Foundation

2008   Received charitable status

Received first grant from Laidlaw Foundation of $38,023

Hired three part-time staff at minimum wage

Programs expanded from four to twelve high schools

Introduced Unity Days workshops, ran first Unity Kickoff Concert final student showcase, and tested first after-school program at Don Mills Collegiate in Toronto

2009   Invited to Halifax to bring Unity Days program to eight schools, national programs launch

Ran first artist educator training retreat in the wilderness with twenty artists

Launched first youth-led leadership group called Uniteam

2010   Moved Unity Kickoff Concert from a small theatre to Yonge-Dundas Square, one of the biggest outdoor stages in the city, booked local headliner Kardinall Offishall

Went to Italy to represent Canada at WeDays conference, sharing best practices

Expanded leadership programs to a group of spoken word artists called Uniffect

Alumni started two new chapters at the University of Western Ontario and University of Toronto

2011 Expanded national program to Western Canada running ten Unity Days programs, first national artist training program, and launched national after-school program

2012 Introduced processes and policies to build a more robust, sustainable organization

Created first HR policy

Co-created two-year strategic plan with staff, artists, volunteers, and board members

Ran first Celebrating Supporters event to engage and thank donors and partners

Invited to run programs in remote First Nations communities in Northern Alberta

2013 Ran first VIP fundraising event and raised over $50,000 (cost was less than $5,000)

Booked first major international headliner Talib Kweli to perform at Unity Festival

Revised Unity's mission, vision, and branding materials

Ran first summer camps giving summer jobs to youth alumni

Signed on national corporate partners and began to segment major funders by program

2014	Started annual staff performance reviews to measure performance and provide feedback
	Staff set goals for what they planned to achieve in relation to organizational strategy
	First time I formally received performance feedback as the executive director
	Introduced health benefits plans for full-time staff
2015	Created trauma-informed dance therapy program funded by Health Canada in partnership with Boost Child & Youth Advocacy Centre and Ryerson University
	Expanded Unity Days programs to British Columbia
2016	Unity created a "theory of change" to define intended impacts
	Refined impact to focus on improving youth mental health by building resilience
	Improved finance systems, adding new processes, policies, and procedures
	Created "Hall of Fame" art piece to acknowledge staff, artists, and volunteers
2017	Experienced anxiety from pressures due to running Unity and family health challenges
	Opened new conversations around mental health at work
	Went to therapy, began to cope, slowly got back on track

Planned a sabbatical, but instead decided to leave Unity permanently

Board hired a non-profit recruiter and created a succession committee and plan

Ran 70 Unity Days programs across Canada, 11 weekly community programs, 8 after-school programs, 4 Unity crew manual programs, and 6 community arts and culture programs partnered with City of Toronto (for a total of 29 weekly programs)

Celebrated ten-year anniversary as a non-profit (as a program, Unity was around fourteen years old)

Ran national artist training summit with fifty artists, elders, and international guests

Revised branding and communications once again

2018   Ran final fundraiser with the team, renamed to Unity Hip Hop Party

Raised over $200,000 and introduced incoming executive director, Rebecca Harrison

My last day at Unity was March 1, 2018

After leaving, I experienced personal grief and anxiety

Launched EPIC Leadership (epicleadership.ca), a social enterprise helping social impact leaders thrive

Married my beautiful wife, Melissa, and got a rambunctiously sweet puppy named Olive

ACKNOWLEDGEMENTS

Thanks to my crew (Maximum Efficiency), my friends, and my art for being there for me through thick and thin. Thanks to Mr. Izumi for connecting schoolwork to something that would change my life forever. Thanks to my older brother Jeffrey who I was proud to call my 'best man' at my wedding and my second player in video games. Thanks to the *entire* Unity family for the vital work they do every day supporting the next generation. To learn more about Unity, go to unitycharity.com

Thanks to the incredibly generous people behind the scenes who supported me throughout the book writing process, including Chris Casuccio, Lynn Brucker, and Suzanne Clark. *Huge* thanks to Don Loney, Jennifer Smith, and the ECW Press team for believing in me and working with me to make this book the best it could be.

A long list of incredibly generous mentors helped build key parts of Unity. There are too many to name them all, but I would like to acknowledge a handful of them here:

Sarah Earl, Shane Green, Matthew Hughsam, Vivian Yeung, and David Wiljer, who provided support with program evaluation

Azim Alibhai and Michael Schlesinger, who developed Unity's mission and value statement

Melanie Chanzy, Christopher Anderson, and Lisa Smecca, who consulted on HR issues

Robin Cory, Anthony Lipschitz, Franklin Garrigues, and Adam Silver, who facilitated meetings on Unity's theory of change and strategy

Stephen Brown and Allison Laux, who helped redevelop Unity's brand strategy

Julian Van Mil, Roman Lifshitz, Damien Nelson, Tiberiu Scrieciu, Abid Virani, Selina Chan, Imad Elsheikh, Erica Cheah, Nikhil Khosla, and Mike Ford, who brought Unity's story to life through design, photo, video, and PR

Ugo DiFederico, Amy Baryshnik, Josh Spagnoletti, Tony Nacev, Monica Yeung, Jen Wan, and Anita Ernesaks, who built budgets, finance processes, and reporting structures

All of the teacher supervisors who generously volunteered their time after school to allow Unity's programs to be possible: Vivian Yeung, Natalie Lapko, Brett Boivin, Nicole Magson, Brian Wendler, Al Karim, and hundreds more

I would also like to acknowledge the staff, artists, and volunteers who helped build Unity. I've done my best to list everyone who contributed two or more years to this important work during my time at the organization.

Aaron Clarfield
Abid Virani
Abigail Demonteverde
Adam Silver
Adit Kiran
Adrian Bernard, a.k.a. "Switch"
Adrian Chan
Adrian John-Chuan
Alannah Belanger
Alexandra Tauhid
Alicia Leung
Ali Muhammad
Allan Rouben
Allen Chung
Amaka, a.k.a. "La Rose"
Amanda Kattan
Amy Baryshnik
Amy Forristal
Anastasia Klyushin
Andel James
Andrew Chung, a.k.a. "Pyro"
Andrew Colantonio
Andrew Harper
Andrew Hicks, a.k.a. "Andycapp"
Andrew Trac
Anthony Gebrehiwot
Anthony Lipschitz
Anthony Rebalbos, a.k.a. "Rein"

Anthony Tse
Armel Njinkeu
Azim Alibhai
Balu
Beatrice Traub-Werner
Beth Horowitz
Bidhan Berma
Bob Blazevski
Bob Veruela, a.k.a. "Boobjester"
Boonaa Mohammed
Branden Taylor
Brendan Pennylegion
Brett Boivin
Brian Chung
Brian Millado
Brittany Badour, a.k.a. "Britta B"
Caerina Abrenica
Cameron Hauseman
Carlos Bustamante
Caroline Fraser, a.k.a. "Lady C"
Casey Stabile
Catherine Turcotte, a.k.a. "Cat"
Cécile Ferandier-Sicard
CG Chen
Charles Mairs Jr., a.k.a. "Killabeats"
Charlie Li
Chris Fernandez, a.k.a. "C-Stylez"
Chris Mustard

Christina Sorbara
Christine Wong
Christopher Anderson
Christopher Nguyen
Clinton Ghosh
Cole Brager
Corey Goldman
Damien Nelson
Damon Murchison
Danielle Olsen
Dan Turcotte
David Delisca
David Forteau
David Gray
David Wiljer
Dawneen Boyle
Dequan Clarke
Diamond Osoteo
Diana Chung
Diana Reyes, a.k.a. "Fly Lady Di"
Drew Moore
Dynesti Williams
Dvij Patel
Elena Ryabova
Ella Avila
Ellen Morgan
Ellen Sue Mesbur
Emelie Carrey, a.k.a. "Sparx"
Emma Smith
Erica Cheah, a.k.a. "E.S. Cheah Photography"

Eric Goldstrand
Erin Zimerman, a.k.a. "Rock"
Ethan Sharer
Faduma Mohamed
Faisal Abbasi
Fernando Campos
Filip Matovina
Francesca Yaskiel
Franklin Garrigues
Galyn Esmé, a.k.a. "NiLLa"
Ghazal Farkhari
Gloria Romy Assé
Grace Premachandran
Greg Villarico
Guillermo Cabrera, a.k.a. "Memo"
Henrick Sales, a.k.a. "Shoolie"
Imad Elsheikh
James Ho
James Luong
Jane Souralaysack, a.k.a. "Psyreine"
Jared Escalante
Jasmine Wong
Jay Harvey
Jendayi Dyer Knight
Jennifer Wan
Jen Tse
Jerome Villa, a.k.a. "Fresh FX"
Jerry Zhao
Jesse Han
Jessey Pacho, a.k.a. "Phade"
Jim Cartasano, a.k.a. "Nastic"

Joanna Boudreau
Joanne Foote
Joaquin Manay
Jodi Weber
Joelle Faulkner
John Choi
John Turley-Ewart
Jordon Veira
Josh Mosher Mandell
Josh Singer
Joshua Spagnoletti
JP Manabat
Julian Van Mil
Julie Wu
Julla Shanghavi
Kareen Wong
Karen Au
Karl Kremer
Karyn Kennedy
Katie Holt
Kay'la Mahy, a.k.a. "Kiki"
Kayin Jeffers
Keane Tan
Kedre Browne, a.k.a. "Bubz"
Kellie Lefaive
Kenneth Goldberg
Kenneth Marzan
Kevin Reigh
Kieon Bisnath
Kimberly Valera
Kizmet

Kosi Eze
Kristine Buerano
Lakesan Savanathan, a.k.a. "Styx"
Lana Feinstein
Lauren Pink
Lisa Smecca
Lishai Peel
Luca Patuelli, a.k.a. "Lazylegz"
Luke High
Lynn Berry
Lynne Mitchell
Mahad Shoaib
Mahal Escandor
Mahindra Ramcharan, a.k.a.
    "Mahnny"
Malik Musleh
Marah Saheb
Marc Chitiz, a.k.a. "Shrek"
Marcel DaCosta, a.k.a. "Frost"
Marcus Lomboy
Marcus Thompson
Mark Cabuena, a.k.a. "Neo Geo"
Mark Holmes
Mark Holt
Mark Siller
Matt D
Matthew Hughsam
Matthew Jones, a.k.a. "Testament"
Matthew Rose
Melanie Chanzy
Melissa Hart

Michael Brobbey, a.k.a. "Fate"
Michael Thomas, a.k.a. "Mike T"
Michael Wen
Mikey Crichton, a.k.a. "Mike C"
Minh Nguyen
Mobi Mawla
Mohab
Monica Yeung
Natalie Lapko
Neeta Dash
Nicole Cheung
Nicole Magson
Nicole Mayari
Nikhil Khosla
Pablo Lopez
Patrick Lum
Pauline Ling
Peter Aceto
Peter Downes
Peter Kozicz
Rachael Edge, a.k.a. "Redge"
Rainer Ramon Plückebaum
Rajni Sharma
Ravi Jain
Ray Abergas
Ray Mendoza
Rei Misiri
Rob Coutts
Robin Cory
Roda Medhat
Roman Lifshitz

Ron Canuel
Roshawn Balgrove
Russell King, a.k.a. "RaSoul"
Ryan Buckspan
Sagar Maria
Salman Baksh
Sarah Dubé
Sarah Earl
Scott Jackson
Selina Chan
Shamar Ramsay
Shane Green
Shawn de Ocampo
Shuo Liu
Stanley Wong
Stefan Tochev, a.k.a. "Introspect"
Stephanie Caldeira
Stephen Brown
Stephen Leafloor, a.k.a. "Buddha"
Sultana Patail
Taeyeon Kim, a.k.a. "TK"
Tafiya Itiaba Bayah
Tanya Kan
Thunderclaw Robinson
Tiberiu Scrieciu
Tiffany Hsu
Tiffany Shum
Tim Morgan
Tina Gong
Tony Chau
Tony Nacev

Ugo DiFederico
Vivek Parikh
Vivian Yeung
Wali Shah
Waris Ali

Weidong Yuan
Weiming Yuan
Wendy Tu
Whitney French
Xolisa Jerome

I did my best to include everyone who was listed on the original Unity Wall of Fame, which was created in 2017. If I missed your name, and it should be included because you contributed more than two years to Unity, or if I misspelled your name, please contact me and I'll take you for lunch as my apology! :)

ABOUT THE AUTHOR

Michael Prosserman found his passion for b-boying (a.k.a., break dancing) at a very young age. By the time he was three, Michael was already standing on his head while watching Saturday morning cartoons.

By high school, Michael was accepted into Cirque du Soleil and was featured in the major motion picture *Honey*. Since then, Michael has had the privilege to share his story, and to perform and facilitate for hundreds of audiences including municipalities, non-profits, corporations, associations, schools, and more, as the founder of Unity Charity (unitycharity.com), an organization using hip hop to improve youth mental health and well-being.

Michael built Unity from the ground up over fifteen years, drawing from his passion for hip hop and mental health advocacy. What began as a small group of volunteers eventually grew to an organization employing eighty staff, raising seven million dollars, and having an impact on the lives of over 250,000 youth. He is a professional speaker who specializes in team culture, development, succession, and start-ups, and he speaks from lived experience, bringing a practical, innovative approach to coaching, consulting, and teaching. Over the past decade and a half, Michael has travelled the world as a competitive b-boy, placing first in over twenty-six battles, and he has facilitated groups from Asia to Europe to the Canadian Arctic. For his work and his dance, Michael has been featured in over sixty major media outlets in Canada including *Maclean's*, *Toronto Star*, *Globe and Mail*, CBC, CTV, and CityTV.

Michael is currently an instructor at the University of Toronto for the Non-Profit Leadership for Impact certificate, and the CEO of EPIC Leadership (epicleadership.ca), a firm focused on helping social impact leaders build sustainable organizations. He also serves on the boards of directors of several charities, including Big Brothers Big Sisters of Toronto, JAYU, and RISE Arts and Community Services. He is committed to empowering leaders in the public and private sector to build resilient, responsive, and responsible organizations.

Purchase the print edition and receive the eBook free!
Just send an email to ebook@ecwpress.com and include:

- the book title
- the name of the store where you purchased it
- your receipt number
- your preference of file type: PDF or ePub

A real person will respond to your email with your eBook attached.
And thanks for supporting an independently owned Canadian publisher
with your purchase!